To my wife, my love and friend, Denise. Thanks for your unconditional love, patience and pointed prose. Thanks for being my support, my encouragement and my number one cheerleader. I love you.

To my beautiful and bright daughters, Amber and Brandi who are quite unique but the same. Thanks for the laughter and love. I love each of you more and more.

And in honor of my Grandfather the late, Sir T.D. Wade, Sr. for his wit and wisdom.

WISDOM FROM GENERATION TO GENERATION

Published by Watersprings Media House, LLC.
P.O. Box 1284
Olive Branch, MS 38654
Contact publisher for permission requests and bulk orders.
www.waterspringsmedia.com

Copyright © 2018 by Fred W. Batten, Jr., All rights reserved.

No portion of this book may be reproduced, stored in a retrieval system or transmitted in any form or by any means (electronic, mechanical, photocopy, recording, scanning, or other), except for brief quotations in critical reviews of articles, without the prior written permission of the writer.

Unless otherwise noted, Bible texts in this book are from the King James Version. Scripture quotations credited to NASB are from the New American Standard Bible, copyright © 1960, 1962, 1963, 1968, 1971, 1972, 1973, 1975, by the Lockman Foundation. Used by permission.

Scripture quotations credited to NIV are from the Holy Bible, New International Version. Copyright © 1973, 1978, 1984, 2011 by Biblica, Inc. Used by permission. All rights reserved worldwide.

Scripture quotations from THE MESSAGE, Copyright © by Eugene H. Peterson 1993, 1994, 1995, 1996, 2000, 2001, 2002. Used by permission of NavPress Publishing Group.

Scripture quotations marked "NKJV" are taken from the New King James Version. Copyright © 1982 by Thomas Nelson, Inc. Used by permission. All rights reserved.

Printed in the United States of America.
Library of Congress Control Number: 2018951466
ISBN 13: 978-1-948877-01-5
ISBN 10: 1-948877-01-5

WISDOM
from
GENERATION
to
GENERATION

by

Fred W. Batten, Jr.

Table of Contents

Introduction 6
Respect the Experienced 10
Skin Deep 12
Clean Up On Aisle Seven 14
There's A Hole In My Bucket 16
Bigger Than A U-Haul 18
Speed Racer 20
PRACTICE! We Talkin' 'Bout Practice 22
Who Left The Gate Open? 24
Double Vision 26
Saved and Sanctified 28
Atmospheric Conditions 30
Deal or No Deal 32
Fight the Power 34
Mr. Rogers' Neighborhood 36
Decent Exposure 38
Blessed Assurance 41
Help Me; Help You 43
Cover the Spread 45
A Case for Censure 47
Huddle Up 49
River of Life 51
Gap Band 53
Wire Service 55
Go Forward 57
Sticks and Stones 59
Book of Learning 61
Shielded by Faith 63
All God's Children Got Shoes 65
Ambassadors 67
Safe and Secure 69
Pass the Biscuits, Please! 71
The Storm 73
The Great Exchange 75
Angel Care 77
Reflections 79
Promises From God 81
The Long Way Home 83
Light Living 85
Political Calculus 87
Parades 89
Principles of Fun 91
Make It Count 93

Which One?	95
"The Youth"	97
Gold Rules	100
He Hit Me First	102
Look! Did You See That?	104
The Elegance of a Christian; Courtesy Counts	106
Social to Save	108
Little Foxes	110
Love: Protects and Promotes	112
Secret to Happiness	114
Never Say Goodbye	116
ABOUT THE AUTHOR	118
CONNECT WITH AUTHOR	121

INTRODUCTION

"If you don't go after what you want, you'll never have it. If you don't ask, the answer is always no. If you don't step forward, you're always in the same place."

— Nora Roberts

"Psychologists tend to agree that wisdom involves an integration of knowledge, experience, and deep understanding that incorporates tolerance for the uncertainties of life as well as its ups and downs."

-Psychology Today

(https://www.psychologytoday.com/us/basics/wisdom)

"Your time is limited, don't waste it living someone else's life. Don't be trapped by dogma, which is living the result of other people's thinking. Don't let the noise of other's opinion drown your own inner voice. And most important, have the courage to follow your heart and intuition, they somehow already know what you truly want to become. Everything else is secondary."

— Steve Jobs

"The wise man in the storm prays to God, not for safety from danger, but for the deliverance from fear. It is the storm within that endangers him, not the storm without."

— Ralph Waldo Emerson

I can remember as a young boy, about seven years of age, wanting to hang around the older folks and listen to them talk. Some of my relatives, as I recall, said that I was an "old head" or an "old man in a young boy's body". In this book I seek to liberate some of the wise sayings that I heard my Grandfather articulate and which ruminated in my mind over the years. My Grandfather, Sir T.D. Wade, Sr. without the title of *life coach* planted seeds in the soil of my life which are bearing fruit some 40 years later. "The wise man must remember that while he is a descendant of the past, he is a parent of the future," observes Herbert Spencer.

Solid is the rock on both sides of the generational divide. Advances in the arts, education technology and self-branding has widened the relational gap between young and old. The divisions extend to racial and economic strains within the greater society. Our families and communities favor the biblical period when the writer chronicles this commentary in Judges 17:6, "In those days *there was* no king in Israel, *but* every man did *that which was* right in his own eyes". Segregated and separatist wisdom leads to isolationism and disjointed attempts to showcase one's abilities to wax elegant in a vacuum. This ought not be. It takes the collective wisdom of the family, village and the church to provide implemental education to the generations.

Conventional wisdom is the belief that what the majority ascribes to is correct. History challenges the success rate of this populace notion of wisdom. Conventional wisdom isn't accurate all the time. Sometimes it is wrong. Millions believed the thought that the earth was flat. Yet, others in Columbus' day believed the earth to be spherical. Paul Rulken observed, "Humans have a bias for groupthink" and are susceptible to taking in flawed assumptions as if they are true.

Traditionally, 30, 40 or 90-day renderings populate the devotion genre. This locks the reader into a specific routine in order to gain optimum benefit. This book, however, supersedes the normal route of a start and finish time. We struggle with timelines and deadlines. Humans have difficulty with the twists and turns of life from one generation to the next. Hence, this devotional, while acknowledging the disconnect among the mature and less experienced ones, draws upon the practical wisdom of my grandfather which he passed on to the eager listeners who were his junior. My grandfather's approach to life, family and God helped shape the insights within this book. He is deceased, now. But his wisdom and his style of communicating the pearls lives on. I have sought to capture his unsophisticated, yet profound philosophy in the pages of this book couched in the framework of the Christian faith. Solomon acknowledges, *"The fear of the Lord is the beginning of wisdom, and knowledge of the Holy One is understanding. For through wisdom your days will be many, and years will be added to your life. If you are wise, your wisdom will reward you; if you are a mocker, you alone will suffer"* (Proverbs 9:10-12, NIV).

The purpose and goal of this book is to stimulate a dialogue between Christians and God, as well as to open the channels of sharing wisdom from generation to generation. This book will benefit you in several ways. It will enhance your quiet time with God. You can also read it as a part of a prayer group, small group, or use it as a discussion starter to ignite conversation among generations.

"The fear of the Lord is the beginning of wisdom, and knowledge of the Holy One is understanding. For through wisdom your days will be many, and years will be added to your life. If you are wise, your wisdom will reward you; if you are a mocker, you alone will suffer."

-Proverbs 9:10-12, NIV

Respect the Experienced

I had the great privilege of growing up around my maternal grandfather. T.D. Wade, Sr. – my Granddaddy – had words of wisdom of which I didn't always understand at the time. He would say things like:

> "Every tub gotta stand on its own bottom."
> "The ground will give what you put in it."
> "People will always be people."
> "Don't hurry through life."

The American culture needs to reclaim the notion of respecting those who are older. We have lost this very important art of generational transfer of wealth to the degree that essential knowledge and skills to survival and flourishing are almost extinct. However, God has kindhearted respect toward the ones seasoned in their years. He says, *"The hoary head is a crown of glory, if it be found in the way of righteous-ness"* (Proverbs 16:31).

Reclaiming this need of generational transfer is nothing new. Cultures from around the world continue to practice this and see the benefits. Japanese honor and respect the elderly members of their society. The Koreans seek the wisdom and knowledge stored in the heart and soul of the experienced parents of their society.

Moreover, America seems to easily discard and discount the wit and wisdom of the more seasoned and experienced generation. This unfortunate reality leaves both generations emptier. The patriarchs and matriarchs age in institutional living with limited and declining relationships with the youthful generation. The younger generation misses out on the invaluable knowledge, insights and experiences of the seasoned giants. This decline of generational transfer is severely impacting the Christian church in America. The moral values and the practice of sound principles are fading fast.

The bridge needs to be repaired, or rebuilt strong enough to withstand the eroding elements of separation and hold the generational transfer of knowledge, wisdom, love, and practical godliness in a fallen and failing society. Standing on this bridge let the experienced saints tell "of battles fought, and victories gained; of burdens borne, and temptations resisted." Let the young think on these things and help "smooth the path of the aged by their courtesy and respect and will bring grace and beauty into their young lives," as mentioned by one Christian commentator.

Passing wisdom from generation to generation is a good thing. *"One generation shall praise Your works to another" (Psalm 145:4, NASB).*

Skin Deep

Beauty pageants are a multibillion dollar industry in America. According to a report released in *Women's News* on January 24, 2016, 2.5 million girls participate in 100,000 beauty pageants each year in the US. America and the World are enamored, fascinated with making the outside look as good as it can. There's nothing inherently wrong or egregious about wanting to look your best. God, our Creator, loves beauty. In fact, God is the Creator of beautiful things. The royal radiance of the sunrise; the majestic serenity of the sunset; the artistic colors of the lilies contrasted against the carpet of green grass are samples of the Creator's love of beauty.

God, in the biblical account of Creation, plants the garden paradise and makes beauty come alive in the persons of Adam and Eve. All things were wonderful, awesome and beautiful, until Adam's disobedience invited sin to place a huge pimple on the face of God's creative masterpiece. Now beauty is not everywhere, but it is in the eye of the beholder. We see others from the surface. For many, beauty is only skin deep. We place more value on the temporary and visible. God, however, is more interested in what's on the inside -- character. No amount of makeup or cosmetic surgery can cover up the bad character caused by the ugliness of sin.

Violence, rape, lying, stealing, gossip, suffering and death are scars that leave human character in hopelessness. It's into this abyss the abundant and extravagant grace of God reaches through the human debris *"to give unto them beauty for ashes, the oil of joy for mourning, the garment of praise for the spirit of heaviness" (Isaiah 61:3).* God has poured upon the human race an unstoppable love, vividly displayed in the beauty of Jesus on the hideous canvas of the blood-soaked Cross. Upon receiving this treasure chest of divine character, the believer passes *"from death unto life" (John 5:24).* In Christ we have beauty. So, *"let the beauty of the Lord our God be upon us" (Psalm 90:17).* The psalmist continues by observing that it is God's graciousness moving upon us whereby heaven and earth gets to observe the works of our hands.

The wily wisdom of my grandfather acknowledged the pendulum beauty swing apparent in the world. However, he insisted in the belief that "hard work never hurt nobody." God hands each one the power and the tools. We are then to cooperate with the Spirit of God in character formation. We are beautiful in the eyes of God!

God loves a character full of beauty. Beauty of good character is deeper than skin deep. Hear the word of God. *"The LORD is more pleased when we do what is right and just than when we offer him sacrifices" (Proverbs 21:3, NLT). "As a face is reflected in water, so the heart reflects the real person" (Proverbs 27:19, NLT).*

Clean Up On Aisle Seven

Have you ever envied the neat and orderliness of a friend or family member? Granddaddy was a master of organization. I remember the layout of the farm. He had hedges over 6 feet tall, stone layered fences lined the north side. Stones from the quarry led one from the driveway to the house. Behind the house to the right was the smokehouse, and approximately 15 yards to the left was the meat hanger. Standing at the fence behind the house one could see the barn about forty yards straight ahead. The outside facility, the outhouse, was to the right on the northern tree line. On the south side of the barn was the garden. Cabbage, okra, snap beans, tomatoes and watermelon is what I recall gathering from the garden.

As I remember, everything was neat and clean. The grass was always cut. Overgrown hedges, I never saw. Oh, then there was the concrete storage house. It was kept neat and orderly. I never saw anything out of place. In grocery stores people pick up items from aisle 3 and lay them down on the shelf on aisle 7. Not so in granddaddy's "store." He would always tell the grandkids, "Put it back where you found it, you will always find it." You probably have heard a variation of this idea. But it takes discipline to do it. I desire better organization like my granddaddy. Right now, as I'm writing, my home office needs a major restructuring.

There are times that our lives can get out of order. The corners of our minds get cluttered. The shoes of our parenting skills get kicked off by the door. Keys of our spiritual life lost in the sofa. Bags of anger and mounds of malice are scattered across our emotional lawns. We find ourselves calling for help and screaming for relief. We turn to self-help books and organizational gurus to sort out messed up lives. When they don't help, we turn up the bottle or pop a pill to numb the pain of broken toys and the scattered puzzle pieces of our lives. This messy, mixed-up world has us trapped. There seems to be no hope.

Our world is maligned and maltreated. Humanity's sin, disorderly obedience, corrupted God's perfect creation. Since then we all like sheep go astray, go our own way due to the iniquity within (Isaiah 53:6). The cleansing and reordering of our offices and houses must start on the inside. The Psalmist David realized this essential truth when he said, *"Create in me a clean heart, O God; and renew a right spirit within me" (Psalm 51:10)*. God did not lose us, but God in the person of Jesus Christ is reconciling the world to Himself (2 Corinthians 5:19). The good news gets better. Luke declares, *"For the Son of man is come to seek and to save that which was lost" (Luke 19:10)*.

There is hope for that which sin caused. Jesus will, and can, reorganize your life. He is willing to put you back where He found you. Let Him do it today.

There's A Hole In My Bucket

If the well was dry on grandfather's property, he would look at the boys and say, "Go fetch us some water." I hated walking the approximately one quarter mile trek to the neighbor's well across the dangerous highway. The reason I disliked fetching water from the well is because I would spill quite a bit walking up the rocky hill back to the house. Each time it seemed like there was a hole in my bucket.

"There's a hole in the bucket, dear Liza, dear Liza, a hole. Then fix it dear Henry, dear Henry, fix it." So, goes the nursery rhyme. Henry can't fetch the water from the well because there's a hole in his bucket. Liza gives Henry instructions, which ultimately required water, to which Henry repeats the fact that his bucket has a hole. It's the holes in our souls and character, which prevents us from being all God wants us to be. It is the small prevarication from the right that goes unchecked which yields a hole in the soul…

We find holes in our clothes that we have stored in the closet. Where did the holes come from? Moths are the culprits. Clothes-moth larvae feed on "wool, cashmere, silk, cotton, linen, fur, feathers, hair, lint, carpets, the bristles of brushes, pet fur and even dust," according to Karl Smallwood in the article entitled, **Do Moths Really Eat Clothes**. They do their work in the dark and in unclean garments. So, it doesn't matter if you are red, yellow, black or white, rich, poor or middle class, the clothes-moth larvae have eaten holes in the fabric of your character. Perhaps the "holy jeans" fashion apparel can be a metaphor for today's lack of Godly character.

Liza told Henry to plug the hole in his bucket with straw. The hole in the garments can be patched; however, a better preventative fix is to have the clothes dry-cleaned. We can close the holes in our souls by practicing a pattern of good thoughts which will lead to right actions. All of which are aided by the sanctifying power of God living on the inside. The best way to close the hole in the clothes of our righteousness is to have Jesus fit us with the *"dry cleaned" robe of His Righteousness which lasts forever (Isaiah 51:8).* To be clear, Jesus by His grace and mercy, fixes the holes in us. We form the character with the resources He provides. Solomon observed, *"Better is a poor man who walks in his integrity than a rich man who is crooked in his ways" (Proverbs 28:6).*

The hymnologist declares, "There is a balm in Gilead to make the wounded whole, there is a balm in Gilead to heal the sin-sick soul." Jesus fills the holes in our hearts, so we can hold fast to the good that He pours in us. In Christ and by His power we can be all that God wants us to be.

Bigger Than A U-Haul

Sitting in that somber space I heard the moans of grief and I saw the tears of loss. Then I heard the minister pronounce, "I've never seen a U-Haul behind a hearse." As a youngster I didn't grasp the meaning. But now that I'm older, I have a better understanding of the concept. The importance of the preacher's words was you can't take earthly possessions with you when you sleep the sleep of death. While it is a fact, in some cultures they bury valuable possessions with their deceased loved ones, the truth is that these items are of no value to the deceased.

Character developed while living on the earth is the only thing that will be of any consequence after one's death. Character is the lifetime work of shaping the quality of the inside so that it can show up on the outside. People admire good character found in others. Character is not reputation. Player X is a good team member on the basketball court, but the same player is always in the newspaper for disruptions ranging from violating team rules to domestic violence. Character is not what you say about yourself. Character is what you do when others are not looking. It is the essence of who you are.

The wise sage on my mother's side would often kid around when he couldn't quite remember the names of the myriad of grandkids. We bounded through the door and with youthful excitement would say hello to Granddaddy. He looked at us with a grin and said, "Who is you?" We would say our names and he'd deny it. We would go back and forth until finally Granddaddy said, "I thought that was you." "Who is you" – has stuck with me through the years. The who in you is bigger than any earthly possession or achievement, it's your character.

Automobiles, old or new, have character. Developed through design, circumstances, events and time the cars character takes shape. In the same way, through trials, time and response, our character is displayed. In the sense that you want a good, dependable car, a good name or character is desirable. For the Christian a Christ-like character as demonstrated in His holy history is the goal.

The possession of good character is invaluable now and in heaven. *"A good name (character) is rather to be chosen than great riches, and loving favour rather than silver and gold" (Proverbs 22:1).*

Speed Racer

Long road trips are one of my least favorite things to do. If I am the driver my knees and back are less enthusiastic than if I'm in the passenger seat. After about three hours or so a stretch break is in order. I, however, enjoy hitting curves at a high rate of speed. There's one particular curve in the city where we live that I hit in a hurry. The Richard Petty race car driver comes out in me.

Too many people are in a hurry these days. Life seems to be one big blur. The progressive moves from the agrarian society to the industrial age to the era of ever-advancing technology that has zapped the western world of what Dr. Richard Swenson calls "margin." In his book he describes margin as "the opposite of overload." That is to say we live such fast-paced lives that we rarely have time to breathe. Once we awaken in the morning we dash to shower, rush to get dressed, rumble down the stairs, run out the door. We then quickly order breakfast in a hurry. Oh, wait we forgot to get the kids up for school. Why are we in so big of a hurry? What's driving us to be the first in line, or to get through the stop light before it changes?

Life without margins or being overloaded with career demands, friendship expectations, church work and academia destroys our ability to breathe. We become fatigued and anxious about everything. The doctors can't figure out what's wrong. It's time to restore margin into the course of your days. I'm reminded of what my Granddaddy used to say every time we would end our visiting. He said, "Don't hurry through life, son. Don't hurry through life." Now, that I've gone through many busy days of my, life I get it. Running full speed ahead on a straight away or rounding the curves will cause damage to the body and mind unless you take time to breathe. Jesus said to his disciples, *"Come aside and rest awhile" (Mark 6:31).*

The fact of the matter is that we all are running fast and furious towards a spiritual burnout. We need to quickly accept the salvation gift that God has given in Jesus. Jesus comes to breathe margin into your life. Today is your day to receive the gift and obey Christ's invitation to rest in him. For spiritual rest and margin Jesus invites you to, *"come to me all who labor and are heavy laden, and I will give you rest. Take my yoke upon you and learn from me, for I am gentle and lowly in heart, and you will find rest for your souls" (Matthew 11:28-29).*

PRACTICE! We Talkin' 'Bout Practice

Allen Iverson played professional basketball for fourteen seasons. Most of which were played for the Philadelphia 76ers. He was a prolific scorer, averaging nearly 27 points per game and he was a good defender. The National Basketball Association voted Iverson Most Valuable Player in 2001. The Naismith Memorial board enshrined the 6-foot guard into the basketball Hall of Fame in 2016. However, many causal sports fans remember Iverson's 2002 interview where he seems to speak despairingly about his *practice* habits.

Anyone who is serious about their craft knows that *practice* is important. Practicing one's craft is essential in order to be good, great, at it. Mozart, a child prodigy of musical genius, would have never been able to compose *Eine Kleine Nachtmusick* I. Allegro without consistent heartfelt practice of the basic and fundamental essentials of his craft. There isn't a musician alive, barring some physical or mental restriction, who does not practice whether solo, in a jam session, or in front of a crowd.

Bill Walton the former UCLA Bruins basketball standout remarked about his first meeting with the outstanding and legendary coach, John Wooden and his insistence on practicing the details of everything basketball and life. Coach Wooden taught his players how to put on their socks to the point he reminded them, "I want absolutely no folds, wrinkles or creases of any kind on the sock." Practicing the details of putting on socks set the foundation for discipline and greatness in basketball IQ and personal character in the John Wooden Bruins'.

Far too often the critique against and the admission by some Christians are that they do not *practice* their faith. Why is this? There may be many variables to this question. However, being takes precedence over doing - practicing the faith. Being in Christ (Romans 5: 1-2) secures our position to perform the law of God through *"Christ in [us] the hope of glory" (Colossians 1:27)*.

The practice of pure religion begins at home before you get to the gym, church, or work. It was a term of endearment that he used to address her, Mama. I never heard my Grandfather speak out of the way towards his wife, my Grandmamma. His verbal affection for her was evident by the way he spoke to her. To this day I have a term of endearment for my love, Denise. One Christian writer from the nineteenth century reminds us that "Christians in the home will be Christians in the church and in the world."

Let us resolve to *be* Christians who live by faith in the Son of God, and *practice* the holy living not by might but by the Spirit of the Lord (Zachariah 4:6).

Who Left The Gate Open?

A story is told about a little dog who thought he was big and bad. He sat on the porch and would run to the fence and bark and growl at the other dogs as their masters walked them. Each day the same ferocious dog barks and hits the fence. One day the big German Shepherd came by and the little dog jumped off the porch barking and growling. Then he hit up against the gate and it flew open. The big dog said, "I've been waiting for this moment." He proceeded to turn that little dog every which way but loose. When he got through, that little dog limped back to the porch and said, "Who in the hell left the gate open?"

Adam's sin opened the floodgates of sorrow, sickness and death upon this earth. Sin caused a disconnection on Earth from Heaven and its peaceful way of life. The passage of each year, month, week, day and hour only heighten the intensity of the ferocious devastation of sin. People and nations attack one another. War, post-traumatic stress disorder and threats of nuclear annihilation have overpowered the fragile good being done in the world. Hope for civility in politics and parenting seems almost lost. Humanity, in its closed, gated cage, fights for survival. It's an unfair fight because humanity's arch-enemy, Satan, *"comes only to steal and kill and destroy" (John 10:10)*.

But the way has been thrown open so that fallen humanity can get from our house back to God's house. Jesus is *"the way, the truth, and the life"* to get to the Father *(John 14:6)*. Sin snapped the power lines of communication. More importantly, God restored the power through Jesus, the Son of Man. The Cross planted at Mt. Calvary over some 2,000 years ago shines the light of an eternal love. Through the empty tomb Jesus opens for us His resurrected gate and path to Heaven.

Our hearts can be glad because, as one has written "the gate of heaven has been left ajar, and the radiance from the throne of God shines into the hearts of those who love Him." Great light flows through the small gap in the gate, now. The gate of salvation is still open. "Now *is* the accepted time; behold, now *is* the day of salvation," according to the apostle Paul in 2 Corinthians 6:2. Greater light will rush through like a mighty river when Jesus comes to rescue His saints and the heavenly gates are open wide as the redeemed of the Lord march into Zion.

I'm so glad Jesus loves me, and the gate of salvation is still open! *"Open to me the gates of righteousness, that I may enter through them and give thanks to the LORD" (Psalm 119:18 ESV).*

Double Vision

Since 1976 during the first weekend in August one can easily have diplopia. Biological twins from across the globe gather in Twinsburg, Ohio for games, fun and "double talk." Others, who are not twins, come to capture this two of a kind binary festival in pictures and video for years to come.

While this double event is profitable to the twins and the town, diplopia is not a good thing for an individual to have. Diplopia is a disorder of vision in which two images of a single object are seen as from unequal action of the eye muscles. We also call it *double vision*. Seeing double or double vision, according to MedWeb, an Internet medical resource, can be caused by excessive alcohol intake, brain tumors, severe dry eyes, this should cause one seeing double to seek medical attention. Diplopia when severe enough can be a life and death situation.

Christians who look in the mirror and see two images of one object may have a problem. Judas the "self-appointed" disciple was a victim of diplopia. Judas associated himself with Jesus, but he was never in association with Jesus. Judas was a hearer of Jesus' words, but never a God pleasing doer of the word. He joined the group to play the role of a disciple of Jesus, but he never allowed the love of Jesus to transform his heart. Like so many people today, Judas saw Jesus, the Great Physician, but he never got to see Him due to his habit of self-medicating. This life of double vision led to Judas' death.

In the 2002 movie, *Catch Me If You Can*, Leonardo DiCaprio portrays Frank W. Abagnale, Jr. a teenager who wrote over 2.5 billion dollars in bad checks by the age of nineteen. He also successfully passed himself off to be a Pam Am pilot, a doctor and a lawyer. Frank lived between two realities. Living in the fun, exhilarating and bad reality caused Frank to end up on the wrong side of the law. Young's Literal Translation of the Bible offers this clear rendering of Mark 8:36, *"For what shall it profit a man, if he may gain the whole world, and forfeit his life?"*

The final vision of God for the Christian is not the instability of a *"double mind" (James 1:8)* nor the *"double tongue" (1 Timothy 3:8)* of a Judas. The optimal vision for the disciple is a single eye fixed on the glory of Jesus our Savior and Lord. It is then that our hope will be rewarded.

"Turn you to the strong hold, you prisoners of hope: even today do I declare that I will render double to you" (Zachariah 9:12). God will give you more than double for your trouble.

Saved and Sanctified

His house was just off US Highway 231. Each day the world whizzed by, but my grandfather managed to survive in a house without indoor plumbing, with well water to drink and rain water caught in a barrel for laundry and bathing. He communicated with friends and neighbors by rotary telephone. His television antenna looked like a silver tree nailed to the side of the house. He never knew the ease in which technology helps and holds us hostage today.

What does social media, online shopping and flying have in common? They help world travelers and local residents pop in and out from place to place in a hurry. Humans haven't always had these luxuries to facilitate an almost instantaneous existence. However, the desire for expediency and efficiency revealed itself in progressive modes of transportation such as; walking, horseback, boat, train, automobile, bus and airplane. Technology has helped to improve transportation and life in general. We get from place to place quicker. We skip waiting in long lines by purchasing the item online. Quick, fast and in a hurry, are the beginnings of a quicker and faster way to live.

This kind of thinking, quick fast and in a hurry, has gained a foothold which is on the way to becoming a stronghold in Christianity. This right-now mentality expresses itself in words such as "I'm saved, sanctified and filled with the Holy Ghost." To some this phrase means that at the moment they receive the salvation gift of Jesus, they are saved and there's no turning back. Others feel this to be a presumptive statement.

Saved, being saved and will be saved are the phases of salvation. We can see salvation, when rightly understood in the following three phases, quick, slow cooker and in an instance. God redeemed and justified fallen humanity in the incarnation, Holy history, death and resurrection of Jesus Christ. The sinner who believes this Good News passes from death to life in Jesus *(John 5:24)* just as quickly as he accepts his new history in Jesus. Phase two is the crockpot stage. In the second phase of sanctification Christ works to deliver us from the power of sin and to transform us into His image. This is the work of a lifetime. The final stage happens in an instance at the return of Jesus. We are saved from the very presence of sin. Believers who died in the Lord will be changed in a moment and in the twinkling of an eye. *(1 Corinthians 15:52)* Believers still alive at the second coming of Jesus will be translated – they move from this sinned cursed world to be with the Lord forever more *(1 Thessalonians 4:16-18)*. This is glorification. The Lord changes our corruptible bodies into incorruptible ones in an instant.

Without boasting or bragging we can humbly say, "I am saved from the penalty of sin by the good news of the Cross of Christ. I am being saved from the power of sin as Christ lives in me. I will be saved from the very presence of sin when Jesus comes to get me – at the second coming of Jesus."

Let's rejoice today in His great salvation. Our salvation is in Him, through Him and with Him!

Atmospheric Conditions

The weather conditions of recent days causes me to be more thankful for dry land. It also causes me to think deeply about life. Watching the weather forecast I heard the meteorologist talk about High-Pressure and Low-Pressure systems. I started thinking. How do these systems affect the weather? What, if any, are the implications or applications for Christians?

At the upper levels of the atmosphere the air converges or moves toward the High-pressure system. Now this makes the cooler air sink or step down because the warmer air is moving away from the High-pressure center at the surface, as a result, we have fair weather. Some Christians are like hot air. They only show up when the weather is fair. They make a grand entrance. Wearing sunglasses, saturated with skin protecting sunscreen and decked in leisure wear, such are ready to be seen. But when it's time to work in the church and serve the community they are nowhere in sight.

The slightly inward moving air in Low-pressure causes air to converge, and since it can't move downward due to the surface, the air is forced upward, leading to condensation and precipitation. It's the cool air Christians that run in to serve, in to worship, in to blessing others. They don't shy away from difficult situations, distressed people or the displaced. They remember that when they were down someone came to pick them up. It's by helping others that the sunshine of God's love and mercy changes the "atmospheric conditions" of our lives and we are able to smile even when our own circumstances are not the best.

As a young boy we didn't have cellphones with weather apps. My grandfather taught me to observe the clouds and which way the leaves turned in the wind. He said if the leaves turned over, then heavy rains were on the horizon. A definite shift in the atmosphere would occur. Today, while the devil is truly busy brewing up storms of low and high pressures, I sense the church needs to reclaim, like the Israelites, the Ark of the Covenant and put it in its proper place in the Temple. It was when they did this that the awe-inspiring cloud of God's Glory chased the priests out of the temple *(1 Kings 8:10-11)*.

The prophet, Isaiah, sensed a need for an atmospheric shift when he declared, *"This is the kind of fast day I'm after: to break the chains of injustice, get rid of exploitation in the workplace, free the oppressed, cancel debts. What I'm interested in seeing you do is: sharing your food with the hungry, inviting the homeless poor into your homes, putting clothes on the shivering ill-clad, being available to your own families. Do this and the lights will turn on, and your lives will turn around at once. Your righteousness will pave your way. The GOD of glory will secure your passage"* (Isaiah 58:6-9 MSG).

Isn't it about time to change the atmosphere? Is it time for the Glory of the Lord to chase us, young and old, out of the high temple praise into the high and low rises to share His love?

Deal or No Deal

Hosted by Howie Mandel the exciting game show Deal or No Deal premiered in America on December 19, 2005. According to an internet source, a "contestant chooses one briefcase from a selection of 26. Each briefcase contains a cash value from $.01 to $1,000,000. Over the course of the game, the contestant eliminates the other cases, periodically being presented with a "deal" from The Banker to take a cash amount to quit the game." Winning Contestants get to share the prize with family, friends and others.

From a different perspective, over a half million people in the great USA are homeless. Barred from bounties' table for selfish decisions or systemic reasons, the poor shuffle between scarce resources and having none, while living in a land of affluence. Why is this so? How did this happen? I hear the stinging voice of some that say, "Jesus said that the poor will always be around." With stagnant wages this statement will remain true. Heaven with clear vision and keen ears sees and hears the plight of the poor.

What should be our response as humanitarians, as our brothers' keepers, and as Christians? Governmental programs aren't adequate enough to sustain this need. Yet, God commands that we deal with the hungry, hopeless and homeless and share our bread, blankets and blessings with them. Sufficient deposits of physical, emotional and spiritual health will increase our meager accounts significantly.

The Old Testament gospel prophet Isaiah reminds the church of its important work presented in chapter 58 verses six and seven. *"Is not this the fast that I have chosen? to loose the bands of wickedness, to undo the heavy burdens, and to let the oppressed go free, and that ye break every yoke? Is it not to deal thy bread to the hungry, and that thou bring the poor that are cast out to thy house? when thou seest the naked, that thou cover him; and that thou hide not thyself from thine own flesh?" (Isaiah 58:6-7)*

Jesus renews this challenge in the New Testament also. A true believer living in the first century or the final century before Jesus' return will help feed the hungry, clothe the naked, visit the sick and imprisoned (Matthew 25:35-40).

Answering this compassionate test of adding value and dignity to the poor tangibly gives good news to the less fortunate in our world. It also helps to meet the gospel command of Jesus. *"Go ye into all the world, and preach the gospel to every creature" (Mark 16:15).*

These commands come from our Lord, Jesus Christ. Are we willing to be a part of this deal? Who's willing to work the deal and be a blessing to others? Deal or No Deal!

Fight the Power

In today's world there are multiple factions and militant groups who prepare, promote and protect their ideological understanding of how the world should work. They live in the country and enjoy the amenities, but their worldview is contrary to that of the larger culture. They march, demonstrate and even hold "torches" to illuminate and bring attention to their demented ideology and warfare.

Some years ago, I heard a preacher observe, "The Church is involved in a great cosmic conflict between Christ and Satan. We are not the Church triumphant, yet. We are the Church militant."

What causes, concerns and worldviews are we fighting for? Are we marching against the injustice of carpet color coordination, or something else? Are we holding the "torch" to enlighten others of systemic bias, poverty and human trafficking? Should the church be concerned about these things or should the church pass these social issues to other groups?

"We wrestle not against flesh and blood, but against principalities, against powers, against the rulers of the darkness of this world, against spiritual wickedness in high places" (Ephesians 6:12).

And this wickedness manifests itself in a variety of ways. However, God has gifted members in each church with talents and ministries, when focused, can fight against and reduce the causalities in their part of the battlefield. The primary battle is indeed against evil and for the Good News of salvation in Jesus. The Church, I believe, cannot stand aloof and allow the social issues of our time to go uncontested seeing that Martin Luther King, Jr., a significant churchman of the 20th century said, "injustice anywhere is a threat to justice everywhere."

On our way to becoming the Church Triumphant, perhaps, it's time to fight unconventionally. Rather than using the selfish strategies and tactics of our culture and chief enemy, we would do well to employ *"every act of justice, mercy and benevolence"* in heaven's arsenal. *"Do not be overcome by evil, but overcome evil with good" (Romans 12:21)*. Christians, in order to make a noteworthy impact, must not only love *"in word and speech, but in action and truth" (1 John 3:18)*.

Fellow Christian believers, it's time to stand up and fight not only against stuff, but for the Cause of Christ. We should stand for the dignity of human life not merely against abortion clinics. We ought to stand for getting treatment for those addicted to opioids and not only against locking up those impacted by the misuse of other illegal drugs. The disciples of Jesus must fight the good fight of sharing the Gospel in an angry world. We can't give up now. I remember hearing it first from my granddad, "Some things you just gotta' fight for."

Mr. Rogers' Neighborhood

My doorbell rang. I went to answer. Upon opening the door, the person began singing these words;

> *It's a beautiful day in this neighborhood,*
> *A beautiful day for a neighbor,*
> *Would you be mine?*
> *Could you be mine?*

It was a good friend who, like me, grew up watching Mr. Rogers' Neighborhood on the Public Broadcasting Station. We laughed and joked about his singing. We also recounted some episodes from the show, the different sweaters that Mr. Rogers wore. I received my first and last singing telegram on that day.

Words, plus music equals a song. Music touches or reaches the "heart", our emotions, while words reach the "head", our minds. Music alone has the ability to adjust or change the mood of the human species. In a 1982 report, consumer psychologist R. E. Milliman concluded that shoppers spent more time and money when the background music is of a slow tempo. Educators use catchy tunes to assist children in learning things like the alphabet and multiplication tables.

The harmonic blend of our words and actions can go a long way in determining the mood of our neighbors. Nice words and kind deeds shared over time helps to deepen the trust and confidence our neighbor will have in us *(1 John 3:18)*. The unfortunate reality, according to a 2010 Pew

Research Center, "nearly one third" of the people surveyed didn't know their neighbors' names.

My Granddaddy could name each of his neighbors within a mile on either side of the road. He believed in good community relations. Maybe it's time, for safety and spiritual reasons that Christians in Jesus' name make beautiful music out of these words;

It's a beautiful day in this neighborhood,
A beautiful day for a neighbor,
Would you be mine?
Could you be mine?
Won't you be my neighbor?

"You shall love your neighbor as yourself. Love does no wrong to a neighbor: therefore love is the fulfilling of the law." (Romans 13:9-10 ESV).

Do you know your neighbor? When is the last time you talked with your neighbor?

Decent Exposure

Some of us parents want to train up our children in the way we didn't get to go. As well-meaning parents, we want our offspring to do more, see more and experience more than we did. So, we buy them culture; piano lessons, summer S.T.E.M. camps, traveling AAU basketball teams and boys and girls club memberships. There's nothing inherently wrong with that premise as long as the things we expose the children to is helpful.

The Law of Exposure states, what you expose yourself to dramatically shapes how you think, feel and act. This law is illustrated by a story.

Once upon a time there was a hunter. One day he went hunting in the jungle and he caught two parrot chicks. Pleased with his possessions he thought he would teach these parrots to talk, and his kids would be very happy to have talking parrots around.

While returning home, one of the parrots managed to escape and flew away to the other end of the forest where there was a sage's monastery. The other parrot was brought to the hunter's home and thus both parrots lived in two different environments.

After a few months, one day, a king was passing by the jungle on his horse. The excruciating heat of the sun tired him and he was thirsty too! He saw one hut and he went there hoping to get some water. It was the place of that hunter. As soon as he entered into the gate, one parrot started shouting from his cage:

"Who's there? Why the hell did you come here? Catch this idiot who is coming here and beat him black and blue."

The king was appalled by the language and went to find water elsewhere. Soon, he reached a sage's monastic village. When the king came closer he was welcomed by a sweet voice:

"You're welcome in this village, Your Majesty! Please come and have a seat. Feel at home here."

The King looked around and he was surprised to see one parrot seated on the roof of the hut welcoming him with a sweet and polite language. After welcoming him, he flew inside the hut to his master and said: *"Teacher, you have an important visitor today. Please take him inside and offer him some refreshment."*

The king was amazed to witness two different behaviors of two parrots. He smiled and understood that good exposure and training always gives different results, and that a man is known by the company he keeps.

The Bible is true. *"Walk with the wise and become wise; associate with fools and get in trouble" (Proverbs 13:20 NLT)*. Parents, uncles, aunts and church members, *"train up a child in the way he should go: and when he is old, he will not depart from it" (Proverbs 22:6)*.

Let us encourage our children to discover gifts and talents and use them to lead, lift and love others to know God. Teach kindness and watch it come back to you.

Exposure today will help to shape, or reshape our future.

Blessed Assurance

My wife asked me the question, "why is our auto insurance so high and it keeps on going up?!" After emailing and talking on the telephone to our agent, I went into the office for a face to face conversation and resolution.

I arrived at the insurance agent's office. He was on the phone. So, I had to wait in a corner chair behind a partition which separated me from the receptionist. The receptionist called my name and my agent met me in front of his office. After the customary handshake I was ready to "get down to business." My statement was, "I need to know why my automobile insurance is so high and it keeps going up?"

He answered in actuarial speak: "Your cars each have different coverage times, your youngest listed insured driver is in a higher risk category. Our records show that you've had a ticket and an accident within the last three years. Lastly, there was a six to eight percent increase in the state last year." Needless to say, I was not a happy camper.

While the Bible teaches that God keeps a record of our sins whether accidentally or deliberately committed, the good news of the Gospel is that Jesus Christ died for the sins of all men and brought salvation, freedom from sin to all men *(Titus 2:11)*. Even if, after receiving Jesus as Savior and Lord, we sin, we can confess our sins to Him and He will cleanse us from that sin *(1 John 1:9)*. It will not be on your record for "three years." The prophet Micah reminds us that

God *"will cast all our sins into the depths of the sea" (Micah 7:19)*. What a blessed assurance.

There's more. In addition to forgiving me of my sins and paying the penalty for my sins, The Lord issues me a reward policy. One writer said, "Every act of love, every word of kindness, every prayer on behalf of the suffering and oppressed, is reported before the eternal throne and placed on heaven's imperishable record." Salvation is a free gift *(Romans 6:23)* to those that receive it. But God will also reward His faithful followers. Look at what I found in the "fine" print of the policy book; *"And, behold, I come quickly; and my reward is with me, to give every man according as his work shall be" (Revelation 22:12)*. That's a blessed assurance! Place your claim today!

In 1873 a musician by the name of Phoebe Knapp, played a tune for Fanny Crosby who was blind from six weeks old. Knapp, as the story goes asked Crosby, "What does the melody say to you?" Crosby replied with what would come to be known as one of the great hymns of the Church, "Blessed assurance, Jesus is mine."

Help Me; Help You

When we save others, we save ourselves. When we help others, our struggle doesn't seem to be so bad. The story is told of a man who had gotten lost in a snow storm. The cold began to freeze his vital signs and his will to live. He heard the moans of another lost traveler. Energy and sympathy revived in him. After much effort he carried his neighbor through the snow drifts to a warm, safe place. They both survived and went on to live productive lives.

Giving and helping others can boost your happiness. Genuine generosity puts others first and helps make you feel good. Giving and helping others registers in the pleasure place in the brain. In one episode of The Discovery Channel's thrilling show, "The Deadliest Catch," one boat hits jagged rocks and begins to sink. The crew and captain abandon the ship and enter the life raft. Still in danger of crashing against the rocks, another boat comes. A crewman jumps in the water and brings the stranded fishermen a life rope. Once the life rope is secured to the raft, the men are pulled to safety aboard the other boat. The captain of the rescuing boat said, "I'm glad we were here to help…I'm just glad everybody's alright." The Good Book declares that *"it is more blessed to give than to receive" (Acts 20:35).*

Your circumstance may be dire and your needs great, but there may be someone else in greater straits than you. God may have you right where you are so that you have the opportunity to hear the distress call of your friend, relative, associate or neighbor. Do you hear the call of that struggling youth, the single mother, lonely senior citizen? If you take the time to help others, God will ensure that a blessing comes your way (Luke 6:38). Writing for Psychology Today, Sara Konrath observed, that "if you want to live a longer, happier, and healthier life, take all the usual precautions that your doctor recommends, and then … get out there and share your time with those who need it."

"Take heed unto thyself, and unto the doctrine; continue in them: for in doing this thou shalt both save thyself, and them that hear thee" (1 Timothy 4:16).

I remember the wise man saying, "Hoping somebody else comes back to hope you." What my granddaddy meant by hope is help. So, to put it another way, "Helping somebody else comes back to help you."

David reminds us when we help and "hope" others we can find help and deliverance from the Lord, [Our] *"help comes from the LORD, who made heaven and earth"* (Psalm 122:2). The opposite effect is also powerfully true as well. Horace Mann observed with acute accuracy that "doing nothing for others is the undoing of ourselves." Take the time to help someone – wife, husband, child, sister, brother, friend or the less fortunate. You will feel better and be better by "hoping" someone else.

Cover the Spread

Romans 5:5 declares that God, through the Holy Ghost, pours His love into our hearts when Christ we received as Savior. If we Christians have, possess, this unconditional love, why are there spirits of unforgiveness, hatred and malice towards other people in the church.

Perhaps the reason for the disconnect is...

My friend Frank is the prankster. My other friend, Mario, is the talker. One day we were all in the kitchen. Mario was pouring Kool-Aid in a cup while telling us another one of his stories. Frank snuck up behind Mario and moved the cup and the Kool-Aid spilled on the counter. God pours but we move the cup, our hearts. Why is this? Is someone playing a prank? Maybe we do not feel worthy of receiving such marvelous love and refuse to be filled with such marvelous love. Therefore, we remain full of the emptiness of a self-centered love that destroys us from the inside. An empty cup is also a thirsty cup.

God pours as we hold our cups in the right position. We are filled with the matchless love of God, a love that makes you love everybody. Feeling good and filled to the brim we put lids on our hearts. Now the lid prevents anything on the outside from getting in and anything on the inside from getting out. This is bad on two fronts. Putting a lid on God's love and keeping it to oneself will cause death by suffocation. Second, putting a lid on our hearts prevents the natural flow of the love of Christ to pour onto the lonely, lowly and the least. This is spiritual death by heart attack, hardening of the arteries.

We must not prevent the agape of God from doing its work in us, changing the contents inside our hearts, and from doing its work through us, flowing out from us to others that they too might *"grasp how wide and long and high and deep is the love of Christ" (Ephesians 3:18)*.

We should be like the little boy at the church potluck who made multiple trips to the juice fountain. When asked why he kept filling his cup, he said, "The pastor told us to ask God to 'fill my cup till it overflows.' But every time I drink it my cup gets empty and I need some more."

In the words of gospel jazz group Take 6:

"Spread love, instead of spreading lies
Spread love, the truth needs no disguise...
More love is what we need."

A Case for Censure

"These are the things that ye shall do; Speak ye every man the truth to his neighbour; execute the judgment of truth and peace in your gates" (Zechariah 8:16).

Breaking News; today cable news reports the intent of three US Congresspersons' desire to censure the president for derelction of duty in not handling the racially charged collision of white supremacist groups and anti-white supremacist demonstrators in Charlottesville, VA. This clash resulted in the tragic death of Heather Heyers. She was run over by an automobile driven by a white supremacist. The castigation of blame on both sides by this nation's elite official caused a backlash of anger to erupt.

Some would argue that the President's insensitivity to the wrongness of his statements seemed to diminish the culpability of the white supremacist groups and erect a moral equivalency is not the only reason why members of Congress want to censure him. I'm inclined to believe that an inability to pass policy through the House and Senate has also added to the environment for censure.

Censure is the legislature's way of issuing a written reprimand to the president so that history will note their displeasure. Aging leadership committees sometimes vote to censure the song and speech of the younger generation, this can be costly. The body of Christ is hurt when battles are fought over preferences while ignoring principles. Paul provides this counsel in Romans 12:10, *"Be kindly affectioned one to another with brotherly love; in honour preferring one another."*

As Christians we engage in being a good neighbor by befriending our neighbors which will help us share the love of Jesus with them. We speak to our neighbors. We are kind to our neighbors. We sit with our neighbors. We share biblical truth with our neighbors. It is when we stop seeking ways to share love with and to our neighbors that we begin to find fault, disparage, and express disapproval of our own brothers and sisters who are reaching souls for Christ. This we should celebrate even if methods differ.

We are more alive and vitalized when we do the work of the church rather than when we merely work for the church. Instead of being the censure police, let us praise God for the good we see in others. Rather than criticize everything others say or do, let us find something to compliment. Rather than condemn others, let us commend them to Jesus. This is the neighborly thing to do. Don't you think?

Huddle Up

They huddled for instruction and information. They broke the huddle full of energy, excitement and ready to *Sound the Alarm*. For several years the American Red Cross has enlisted the help of individuals and community organizations to spread the news of fire safety by going door to door to save lives by installing free smoke detectors and batteries.

The need for this campaign is great because "an average of seven people die every day from home fires in this country," according to Gail McGovern, president and Chief Executive Officer of the Red Cross. Gifting the community residents with home delivery of the smoke detectors has been reported to have saved 258 lives since the program launched in 2014.

Jesus huddled with and instructed his disciples on how to reach the lost. The disciples watched as Jesus prayed for, mingled with, and brought glad tidings to the lonely, comforted the broken-hearted and healed sin sick souls. Jesus, after His death and resurrection, gathered his followers and charged them to *"Go ye into all the world, and preach the gospel to every creature" (Mark 16:15)*. They huddled and waited for the promised power of the Holy Spirit. The Spirit came. The disciples armed with Jesus' example and commission broke the huddle and carried the Gospel to their world.

The church huddles for worship and the word. While millions still haven't heard the powerful Good News, we hear of in fighting, backbiting and church splits. The body of

Christ is fighting, brother against brother and sister against sister. When I told Granddaddy that I wanted to fight my friend across the highway his wisdom went like this. "If you go to bopping his head and he go to bopping your head, what kind of sense does that make?" Maybe it's time to remember and repurpose the reason for the gathering of the church to include serving one another, *(Galatians 5:13)* loving one another *(John 13:34)* and *"forgiving one another" (Ephesians 4:32)* in addition to witnessing the saving grace of Jesus to those outside of our huddle.

Teams huddle on the sidelines for instruction, inspiration and insight. To stay in the huddle means to implode and forfeit the chance to win the game by executing the right play. Churches huddle in prayer for instruction, inspiration and insight. Refusing to leave the huddle believers forfeit the chance to help someone. It's time to break loose from the building, the familiar, the potlucks, and the paralyzing fear. A large number of people who will never come to hear the gospel are waiting for the Good News to come to them.

Families scatter without a prayer huddle. Children gain inspiration from music, movies and video games. It might be time to huddle at the dinner table, again. What would it hurt to huddle and *"seek first the kingdom of God?" (Matthew 6:33)*

River of Life

Just to the right of the barn was a patch of trees which opened to a wonderland. Here we found relief from the summer heat as we splashed and drank from the babbling brook of cooling water. The refreshment value that Granddaddy's stream added to us kids was immeasurable.

Are you a plus, or a minus in the lives of the people that you lead? Are you a giver or a taker? Do you add value (bless) to others or do you subtract/extract value (blessings) from others?

A negatively contagious person or leader is like a stagnant pond that takes in without an outlet. The Dead Sea or Salt Sea located between Jordan and Israel is the lowest land elevation on Earth. This body of water receives water from the Jordan River in the north. Without an outlet and its very high salinity no appreciable life is able to live there. Takers aren't concerned about the welfare of others. They are negative when it comes to being other-minded. Biblical counsel to *"Don't look out only for your own interests, but take an interest in others, too" (Philippians 2:4 NLT)*, is virtually ignored. This type of person breeds selfishness and breathes sickness into the atmosphere. Death will soon come to such a person's leadership, ministry or influence.

A positively contagious person/leader is like a mountainside stream that gives and refreshes others. Look, for miles around the trees grow, the flowers decorate the terrain while reaching up to the sun, fish swim and deer hydrate. This person is like water in dry places. Others grow and thrive from the spirit of giving. But that's not all. The giver also benefits. *"Give and you will receive. Your gift will return to you in full – pressed down, shaken together to make room for more, running over, and poured into your lap. The amount you give will determine the amount you get back" (Luke 6:38 NLT).* Jesus is the ultimate giver. He gave up heaven, came to earth, healed the sick, and then died on the Cross. What blessings and value has been added to our lives because "There Is a Fountain Filled with Blood."

A reservoir reserves and contains and conserves, while a river provides and promotes life upstream and downstream. As John Maxwell says, "Be a River instead of a reservoir."

Gap Band

Let's just be honest, there is a gap between generations. The gap shows up in the matter of home training - that is to say, the way parents raise their children. This is not all bad. There needs to be a chronological difference between the age of parents and children for a host of reasons which would include maturity.

Now among the differences we could cite music styles, fashion, technological literacy, and certain particularities regarding children and discipline. If you are over fifty you were taught to say, "Yes, sir" and "No Ma'am" to any adult without regard to their family connection. Today, it seems that that courtesy and level of respect has skipped a generation. A few days ago, I heard a teenager reply to her mother, "I said, yeah."

My homegrown, over fifty training rose up inside of me and screamed, "Unacceptable."

While some gaps between the generations may be small and insignificant, some differences are huge and significant and may cause societal consternation. But a little bit of home training based on biblical principles can go a long way in helping all generations to be better persons in a mixed-up world. The Israelite parents never knew what their daughter would grow up to be. But in Syria many miles from her home this little maid was a witness for home training which includes knowing the God of the Bible. She had a spiritual base. She knew where to find natural and spiritual healing.

She pointed Naaman the seriously ill Syrian military leader to the prophet of God. In so doing Naaman received healing.

We may not know the extent to which our teaching will help our children. We must bridge the knowledge and wisdom gap separating our generations. How? Society can close the gap by governmental-funded programs like President Barack Obama's Fatherhood Initiative, faith-based groups providing formalized rite of passage activities or by informal, yet intentional, planting seeds of wisdom by parents, grandparents and others into the lives of the next generation. Mutual respect and understanding can be a reality. *"And he will go on before the Lord, in the spirit and power of Elijah, to turn the hearts of the parents to their children and the disobedient to the wisdom of the righteous – to make ready a people prepared for the Lord" (Luke 1:17 NIV)*.

Placing our confidence in the Word of God let us, *"Train up a child in the way he should go: and when he is old, he will not depart from it" (Proverbs 22:6)*. "The ground will give ya' what ya' put in it," said Sir T. D. Wade, Sr. The ground of your mind will yield the seeds you put in it. *"Give, and it shall be given unto you; good measure, pressed down, and shaken together, and running over, shall men give into your bosom" (Luke 6:38)*.

Wire Service

Why does he act that way? What's wrong with her? Why does she behave in such a hateful manner? Temper is a by-product, at least in part, of one's temperament. Temperament theory suggests that there are four basic types of people; choleric, phlegmatic, melancholy and sanguine. Choleric is fast and dominate. Phlegmatic is steady and easy-going. Melancholy is analytical and wise. Sanguine is bubbly and a people person. These personality traits manifest themselves as blends, that is to say, we are not only one temperament but a combination. Thus, the way we are "wired" determines how we think about things, how we feel about life and how we react to stimuli.

How we respond or react to life has much to do about how we're raised. If your parents were "yellers" you will reflect that or retreat from it. If love and support existed in your home you will most likely demonstrate similar attributes around others outside the home. Ellen White suggests, "The truth lived at home makes itself felt in disinterested labor abroad. He who lives Christianity in the home will be a bright and shining light everywhere." The Bible challenge is that we love one another. Such seeds of love sown and displayed at home will show up abroad and at work, at school and at church. *"Now, God himself and our Father, and our Lord Jesus Christ, direct our way unto you. And the Lord make you to increase and abound in love one toward another, and toward all men, even as we do toward you" (1 Thessalonians 3:11-12).*

God created you for His glory *(Isaiah 43:7)*. God placed within you a desire to succeed and follow what Rick Warren describes as your SHAPE. This acrostic means Spiritual Gifts, Heart, Abilities, Personality and Experiences. God has hard-wired you to experience life through the prism of your SHAPE. Light that shines through a prism adds color to its surroundings. *"The path of the righteous is like the morning sun, shining ever brighter till the full light of day" (Proverbs 4:18).*

Dr. Oswald J. Smith used to say, "The light that shines the farthest will shine the brightest at home." What you do inside will eventually show up outside. Don't miss the double entendre.

Go Forward

The rain didn't stop the outdoor concert. The excited crowd exceeded the planners' expectations. Many concert goers parked in the grassy area to the left of the stage. After the concert ended it started to rain again. Sam was one of the unlucky ones. His couldn't go forward. The car couldn't gain the traction needed. The tires kept spinning in the mud. Sam needed some assistance to get out of this predicament. Fortunately, there was a man with a truck who helped Sam's car get out of the mud and to go forward.

Being stuck in a situation and unable to go forward isn't the best? Have you ever been there? Have you ever wanted to go forward in that business deal but something held you back? Have you ever felt like the walls of your relationship were closing in on you and you were trapped? Going forward under these conditions can seem impossible. This was the experience of the newly delivered Israelites. God by His mighty power removed them from Egyptian slavery. Now, they are at the Red Sea with mountainous terrain on the left and right. To make matters worse Pharaoh changed his mind and was in hot pursuit to reclaim them as slaves. What shall they do? What can they do? Fear overtook the people. They saw no way out. They felt like they were going to die.

It's at this moment that Moses prayed to God. Moses, like us prayed when faced with confined and constricted spaces, Moses wanted to know what to do. God's reply, "Stop praying to me. Trust me. Go forward!" There are times, or there will be times when we feel stuck, cornered by our past, desperately trapped by environmental conditions. And God tells us to do something or go forward into what seems like suicide. It was at the moment of complete trust that Moses and the children of Israel saw the miracle power of God make a way out of no way. God made a highway through the Red Sea. It is a forward faith that gives you victory and allows you to see the fate of your enemy. "Gotta keep pushing to get to the other side," said my hoary sage.

And God said, *"Speak unto the children of Israel that they go forward" (Exodus 14:15).* What is holding you back from pursuing that God-sized dream, career move, that relationship? Is it fear of failure? John Maxwell observed that we ought not to let failure stop us. He made the following observation, "Failing forward is the ability to get back up after you've been knocked down, learn from your mistake, and move forward in a better direction."

You've been standing in that same spot for days, months, years or decades. What's holding you back? The mud has dried by now. Shake your atrophied legs and start walking by faith in the Word of God.

"But the Lord says, "Do not cling to events of the past or dwell on what happened long ago" (Isaiah 43:18, Good News Translation).

Sticks and Stones

One day I saw two young boys who were no more than 10 years old playing in the front yard. They each had sticks approximately three feet long. They were using the sticks as swords. I could hear the clashing of each blow. Fencing is the sport which this event reminded me of. I am fascinated with fencing, with the head gear, the suit, the back and forward dance of the competitors and the bayonets.

Unlike the two boys battling with sticks and fencers we are in a real battle. Scriptures alert us to the immense pressures and stressors of the fight between good and evil, Christ and Satan. Every man, woman, boy and girl are in this fight. Make no mistake this war is for real. Just as in any fight you need the proper weapons. In WWII the Allied forces were facing difficult times in the fight against Hitler and Axis power. The decision to drop the atomic bomb was the result of serious deliberations. The United States and the Allied forces defeated the Axis of Evil, The world was a better place without the evilness of that regime.

The arrayed battlefield is against you. Each day the enemy strategically places booby traps, snipers and artillery to wound, maim and destroy you. He launches doubt to break confidence. Deception hurls at hiding the truth that you are more than a conqueror in Jesus *(Romans 8:34)*. Fear, like out of nowhere, comes from the sniper's gun to paralyze forward faith. Let's remember that we have Jesus who successfully navigated through this battlefield before and he promised to fight the battle for you, with your cooperation. *"Thus saith the Lord unto you, Be not afraid nor dismayed by reason of this great multitude; for the battle is not yours, but God's"* (2 Chronicles 20:15).

I see two people fencing, Satan lunges towards you. You parry his strike with the shield of faith. In your hand is *"the sword of the Spirit, which is the word of God"* (Ephesians 6:17). Your enemy flinches and your riposte is successful. Stay alert! Don't relax! But wait, as I look closer, I am no longer able to recognize you. It looks like *"Christ in you, the hope of glory"* (Colossians 1:27). Your continuous feeding on the Word of God has produced fruit.

It's like my Grandfather said, "the ground will give ya' what ya' put in it." Your life will give you what you constantly give it. Sow sticks of self-doubt and the garden of your mind will yield the fruit of an insecure person. Sow stones of unforgiveness and your heart will begrudge others and leave your soul vacant of love.

Christ delivers the final lunge and hits our fiercest enemy. Satan will cry out, "Touche!" In fencing, touché means that the opponent scored a hit or wound. Keep fighting the good fight, my fellow fencers. One day the great dueling will be over and *"at the name of Jesus every knee should bow, in heaven and on earth and under the earth,"* (Philippians 2:10) with Christ we win!

Book of Learning

There are many marketing their webinars, podcasts and books. It's all over the place. We find the evidence of marketing on the radio, television, Facebook, and Google just to name a few. They all tell you how much you will benefit from their products. That's what marketing is supposed to do. It's supposed to sell you, convince you of your need of the program or product. People, businesses and organizations spend millions of dollars to either increase or maintain their market share. They do so expecting a return on the investment.

The marketing strategies of many of the products and ideas of today will be obsolete. The passing of time will diminish the usefulness, effectiveness and efficiency of many products in their present form. Companies manufacture their products to last a measured time upon which they need replacing. There is one divinely inspired and originated product assembled by human hands that is timeless in its inspiration, influence and impact upon the whole of history. I speak of the Bible, the Holy Scriptures. Bishop William Hobart Hare observed concerning the durability and relevance of the Book, **"Here Is an Anvil That Has Worn Out Many A Hammer."**

What are the benefits of reading the Bible? What will you gain from opening the pages of the Holy Scriptures? God the Father, God the Son and God the Holy Spirit coordinate the marketing of this story, saga, and salvation documentary. My Granddaddy, with limited education, believed in the power of the living Word of God. He said, "Do what the Good Book says, and you will do good." The benefits one receives by reading and applying the principles contained in the book are immeasurable. Here are just a few things you will get from reading this book:

- Knowledge of the loving character of God
- Wisdom to apply truth
- How to pray and get an answer
- Salvation from sin
- Sabbath rest in a hurried world
- Peace that passes all understanding
- Time honored stories full of grace and truth

All of these and much more will be yours as the Spirit of God loads you with His benefits *(Psalm 68:19)*. *"For whatsoever things were written aforetime were written for our learning, that we through patience and comfort of the scriptures might have hope" (Romans 15:4)*. The Holy Scriptures by many accounts is the most purchased book historically. Yet, its readership is still lacking. The new pastor was asked to teach the junior high boys' Bible class in the absence of the regular teacher. He decided to see what they knew, so he asked who knocked down the walls of Jericho. All the boys denied having done it, and the preacher was appalled by their ignorance.

In order to reap the benefits of God's Word, Christians must return to being "people of the Book."

"Study to show thyself approved unto God, a workman that needs not to be ashamed, rightly dividing the word of truth" (2 Timothy 2:15).

Shielded by Faith

The shield of faith is the next piece of the armor of God that each individual Christian needs, as well as the collective body of the Church. Faith is the reality that believers are leaning, putting their full weight and confidence in the power, capacity and ability of God to bring them out.

The apostle Paul encouraged the saints in the Ephesus church to *"above all, taking the shield of faith, wherewith ye shall be able to quench all the fiery darts of the wicked" (Ephesians 6:16)*.

He knew from personal experience life's unexpected and sudden storms from the enemy have a way of testing the believer's faith in Christ. It is here that taking up the shield of faith allows one to deflect the fiery darts, defend the heart and disrupt the enemy's momentum. In so doing this allows us to strike a blow.

The ancient Roman military made use of a very creative, incredibly valuable tactic that made use of their large shields. The opposition forces would shoot arrows of fire and launch stones and other projectiles. With exact precision "the soldiers would close ranks into a rectangular array – called the *testudo*, or 'tortoise,' formation—and those on the outside would use their shields to create a wall around the perimeter" according to freebiblestudyguides.org. Then those in the middle would raise their shields over their heads to protect everyone from airborne missiles. This rectangular configuration of humans and raised shields resulted in a virtually unstoppable defensive force.

Like Granddaddy said, "Some things you just can't do alone." Every year in September or early October before the rains came Granddaddy would say, "It's time to go to the woods." Able-bodied men and boys would take chain saws and axes to hunt firewood for the winter.

When the seasoned members and the youngsters of families and churches rally around one another and raise the shield of the Christian faith, a virtually unstoppable force will emerge. They will be able to stand against the good for nothings and misguided people hurling accusations, belittling and using coarse words. With the shield of faith in hand the church will also be a mighty fighting army. Like Nehemiah's working warriors we must fight and rebuild the broken walls of the city, church and our families. The enemy of Good will come to distract and disrupt, but we must say like Nehemiah, *"I am doing a great work and I cannot come down" (Nehemiah 6:3).*

Raise the shield of faith! Fight the good fight! Victory is only 52 days away!

All God's Children Got Shoes

We always had food on the table, clothes on our backs and shoes on our feet. Mom and Dad worked two jobs just to make ends meet. We were poor and we knew that others had more. I was in fifth grade gym class. Someone talked about my sneakers. They said that my shoes made loud clapping noises when I ran across the gym floor. They even mocked that my shoes were like skates, meaning that I would slide some ways before I would come to a complete stop. This hurt me. This was the first time I paid attention to sneakers, gym shoes. I immediately began to petition my mother about getting better gym shoes. I even went as far as shoe sabotage to convince her that I needed a better gym shoe. It worked! I got another pair of the same type of shoe.

It wasn't until middle school when I made the basketball team that I was able to wear one of the brand name athletic shoes, Converse. By virtue of making the team I received a pair of gold colored Converse - All Star, high tops. I was so proud that I made the basketball team. But I was equally happy to have a better-quality shoe to wear. My feet would never again clap the floor or feel like skates. I could run and stop with the best. I had the right shoes on my feet.

Today, people, men, women, boys and girls, are running in circles. Families can't seem to be able to stop. There is an epidemic of violence, sexual misconduct, murder, addiction and human suffering. The pace of such dysfunction and sin is quickening. People are asking for help from the political systems but that promised help is not coming fast enough. Yet, the hope and help the world needs is present and resident in the feet of the Christian Church. The Gospel properly carried, rightly understood, and received brings peace to the troubled heart.

I can hear him humming a tune as he prepared his shoes for a spiritual convocation. There he sat amidst the shoe polish, horsehair brush and shine cloth and his special shoes. He was fixin' to go somewhere. Granddaddy T. D. Wade kept his shoes in good repair. Even his work boots looked good. As I think about how he stewarded what he had, I feel somewhat guilty for neglecting to practice better care of my shoes and other earthly possessions.

It's time for, fellow believers, to put on the best shoes ever made. *"And your feet shod with the preparation of the gospel of peace" (Ephesians 6:15)*. Put on your Gospel shoes. Forget about yourself. Reach out to others and see what the grace of Christ will do through you. *"The Spirit of the Lord is on Me, because He has anointed Me to preach good news to the poor. He has sent Me to proclaim freedom to the captives and recovery of sight to the blind, to set free the oppressed" (Luke 4:18)*. With the right shoes on we can bring peace to our world.

Ambassadors

I would smile when I saw Andrew Young, Jr., an African American, with the title of Ambassador. In this position he represented the government of the United States of America to the United Nations. His job was to forge relationships with diplomats at the United Nations as well as convey the policy positions of the United States. As much as I, a black boy from the south, admired Ambassador Young, I was excited to know that Edward Dudley appointed by President Franklin D. Roosevelt in 1949 became the first African American ambassador of the United States.

The ambassador represents the interests of his country and seeks to extend goodwill to another country. Ambassadors are evaluated by whether they foster better relations and maintain good relations or not. My mother who got it from my grandfather often reminded us that we represented our household, our values and the family name. She expected my siblings and me to "dress right," "talk right," and "do right." Mother wanted us to be nice to others, speak well to, and of others. She didn't want us spending money we didn't have on the latest fashion, but to take care of what we had. As children we were ambassadors of our household to the outside world.

Jesus Christ sought to extend His work upon the earth through the church. It is the members of the church who are chosen to be Christ's ambassadors to the world. *"Now then we are ambassadors for Christ, as though God did beseech you by us: we pray you in Christ's stead, be ye reconciled to God." (2*

Corinthians 5:20) Because this fallen world still needs love, joy, and someone to believe in, the church still has work to do. Since marriages are still ending in divorce, teenagers are running away from home, leaders lack integrity and hurt people are still hurting other people, the church must rely on the power of the Holy Spirit to properly and appropriately present Jesus, our best and only help (Acts 4:12).

Hey, church, (pastor, elder, bishop, deacon, pew members) let's be that ambassador in whom God is well pleased. It's time to lift Christ, not our individual causes of self-interest. Jesus said it best, *"And, if I be lifted up from the earth, I will draw all men unto me" (John 12:32).*

Safe and Secure

I have three girls in my house – my wife and two daughters. Their safety is a big concern for me. Now that they are older and traveling to and fro, my concerns are elevated because there are so many threats to one's safety and security. So much so, that when either of the girls returns to their homes at night they are to call me or their mother so that we can talk them safely into the apartment with door locked and alarm set. If either of us are traveling via train, plane, bus or car we group text time of departure and as soon as we arrive at the destination another text is delivered.

While reading a devotional the other day the author made this statement, "As soon as there was sin, there was a Savior." This reminded me of the fact that God is concerned about my spiritual safety and security. Sin separated human beings from the tranquil relationship with God. Sin disrupted the peace between God and humans and created an emergency crisis. But this crisis did not catch God by surprise. Before the first "a" in as, and the last "s" in the last as could be thought, God's plan of salvation was activated. God made His promise in Genesis 3:15 come alive by stating that Jesus would come and win the war against Satan. Substantiated by the Word of God this plan is eternal. God secured our relationship with Him through the life of Jesus which was *"slain before the foundation of the world" (Revelation 13:8)*.

Sometimes, when I am traveling alone, I forget to contact my girls to tell them I made it to my destination safely. My memory lapse is met with an arresting text reminding me that others love me and are concerned about my personal safety. God, the Father, God the Son and God the Holy Spirit is concerned about getting you from your house to His house. As you board this Gospel train headed for heaven, be on the lookout for some divinely ordained text messages along the way.

> *I love you with an everlasting love (Jeremiah 31:3).*
> *I will never leave you nor forsake you (Hebrews 13:5).*
> *Christ says to us that we are more than conquerors (Romans 8:37).*

My prayer is as soon as your feet strike Zion that you will receive a great welcome from the angels, other redeemed saints like Abraham, Isaac, Luke and Timothy. But once you see Jesus and receive His royal welcome you will feel safe and be at rest. I'm confident that you will look around and find all things well!

Dr. Martin Luther King, Jr. envisioned an end to racism, violence and injustice in America. His dream would culminate in these words, "Free at last, Free at last, Thank God almighty we are free at last." I too have a dream that sin and all its appendices will be defeated. Our turbulent journey ended. We disembark on Heaven's shores. Home at last, Home at last, Thank God almighty, we will be home at last!

Pass the Biscuits, Please!

On Sunday mornings my mother would go into the kitchen, rearrange the countertop, spread flour on the countertop and make homemade bread. I would watch as her brown hands turned white from the flour and water mixture. From time to time she let me play like I was a baker. I helped knead the dough, roll the dough and put it in the preheated oven. It was fun. The best fun was eating that wonderful hot biscuit with butter or grape jelly or eating it by itself.

Another part of the bread making process was watching the "magic" dough rise or get bigger. Mother would often send me to the neighborhood grocery store to get baking yeast. I did not know that this was the "get bigger" agent that made the dough rise! Wow, I didn't know that my mother and I were applying the law of the leaven found in the Bible – *"The kingdom of heaven is like unto leaven, which a woman took, and hid in three measures of meal, till the whole was leavened"* (Matthew 13:33).

Jesus uses the leaven or yeast in the meal or flour as a description of how God's Grace works. As I peeked over the counter I would try to catch the dough rising. I would go outside and come back in and the dough had risen. That's magic. The Grace of God received in life isn't magic but it "works secretly, silently, steadily, to transform the soul," as one writer suggests. It is Grace, the Spirit of Christ, which empowers us to rise above bigotry, to get bigger than bad words and bad behavior in our lives and the lives of others.

When we want to retaliate against insensitivity and injustice grace helps us respond appropriately. *And He said to me, "My grace is sufficient for you, for My strength is made perfect in weakness." Therefore, most gladly I will rather boast in my infirmities, that the power of Christ may rest upon me" (2 Corinthians 12:9 NKJV).*

May the Grace of our God empower you to love the unlovable, help the hurting and in so doing you will obey the law of the leaven. Others will notice the change that God is making in you and will want what you have. They too will say, "Pass the biscuits, butter and grape jelly, please."

The Storm

The storm rumbled through my town. Lightning hit a transformer and all the electricity went out. The meteorologist predicted bad weather for several days. I had intended to get some candles and batteries earlier in the week but I didn't. So, I had to feel my way through the house to where we kept the flashlight. I was hoping that the batteries were still good. I pushed the button and "there was light." I was totally relieved and thankful that my Ever-Ready batteries lived up to their name and hype.

Storms of various degrees of intensity and volatility are a frequent part of the annual cycle. Electric, thunder, tornado and hurricane are the typical storms that ran across the terrain of the USA. These storms hit communities with loss of property, persons and pictures. The significant impact of storms upon humans prompted one preacher to say, "We are either in a storm, coming out of a storm or going into a storm." So, the important thing is to be ready. Preparation helps one navigate through seasonal storms of life.

When Jesus came to this world the deafening darkness engulfed His creation. Satan had managed to tarp the world's citizens with thick clouds of disobedience and disregard for God and moral correctness. Earth's inhabitants did what was right in their own eyes. Satan claimed to be the "prince and power of the air." To this darkness Jesus came ever ready to shine, impart and give the light of truth, kindness and love. At every moment Jesus was ready to touch the bowed down, to hear their faintest cry and die a sacrificial death as Savior.

It is in this light that we stand. With this light the church is to be ready at all times to *"preach good tidings unto the meek; to bind up the brokenhearted, to proclaim liberty to the captives, and the opening of the prison to them that are bound; to comfort all that mourn"* (Isaiah 61:1-2). The readiness of the church depends on the readiness of individuals in the church to receive Jesus, the true Light of the world. It's then that we are ever ready to hold up the light when the storms of disaster, devastation and dread strikes any neighborhood in the world.

How's your spiritual battery? Are you ever ready to shine for Jesus? How long has your light been on the shelf? Arise for your light has come not to shine in the face of your neighbor, but onto his pathway and into his life?

But this I call to mind, and therefore I have hope: The steadfast love of the Lord never ceases; His mercies never come to an end; they are new every morning; great is your faithfulness. *"The Lord is my portion, says my soul, therefore I will hope in him"* (Lamentation 3:24).

The Great Exchange

The retired minister sat across the table from the young, energetic pastor. The old cleric had watched the young preacher grow up from his youth. Now, this old preacher who had served in the church as a teacher, pastor and administrator recalled in a moments time the emotions that overwhelmed him as a "wet behind the ears" pastor. He also successfully completed various building projects and served on several impactful committees. This well-beloved and much respected minister said, "I'm honored that you asked me to be your mentor. I have but one request."

"Anything you want, sir," replied the wide-eyed neophyte with a smile.

"Okay, here's the deal. I will share all I know about ministry, leading people, administering the business of the church and such things. You promise to keep me abreast of the theological landscape and discussions happening in today's world."

The new preacher said, "Yes, sir. You've got a deal!"

Which of these two ministers got the better deal? Who would benefit the most from this exchange of ideas, from this mentoring relationship? Well, I must confess that I have been blessed and benefited tremendously from the sage and student mentoring relationship. However, I'm not sure how much I contributed to my mentor's knowledge of the theological debates and grappling because he seemed to be pretty aware of them.

I hear my grandfather saying, "A tub gotta' stand on its own bottom." This sentiment is true in the sense that everyone should work hard and pull their weight. The reality is that no one makes it to the top without help. Moses received help from Jethro. Elijah mentored Elisha. Paul exchanged his sage wisdom for Timothy's youth and energy.

Sin caused spiritual bankruptcy to fall upon humanity. The human race was plunged into darkness and condemnation under law. Depression, drought and defeat resulted. The marred and maligned image of God in humans resulted. All seemed lost. But God came looking for His creation in the Garden of Eden in the cool of the day (Genesis 3:9). Grace, God's unmerited love helped undeserving people. Human beings, through the great Seed promise, (Genesis 3:15) exchanged forgiveness, peace and power for the sinner's disobedience, guilt, shame. Jesus, the promise, became the reality. Jesus restored our relationship with God. Jesus took our sins upon Himself. Jesus died so that we can live. Who benefits from this great exchange, in that while we were yet sinners Christ died for us? (Romans 5:8)

As you think back over your life, how have you benefited from the Grace of God? How does that make you feel?

Angel Care

Angels we have heard on high
Sweetly singing o'er the plains
And the mountains in reply
Echoing their joyous strains

Angels we have heard on high
Sweetly, sweetly through the night
And the mountains in reply
Echoing their brief delight

These are the glorious words that the Angels did sing to announce and declare the birth of Jesus, the Savior of humankind. This may very well be the favorite angelic encounter of many with humans. We are thrilled and afraid along with the shepherds as they are surprised by this strange encounter with the heavenly being.

It is, however, not the only experience of its kind. The Scriptures detail other accounts of how Angels have entered into the human experience to communicate a Divine intervention and message to help save or protect God's salvific plan and thwart Satan's disruptive attempts. The Bible tests the faith of the believers by interjecting angel stories as additional protection from danger. Such protection is like security measures that homeowners have used over time. The security evolution of the American homeowner includes the "white picket fence," a barking dog, security lights and a monitored security system as their layers of personal protection. Yet, these forms of security cost. The fence will need more paint. The dog will need food and veterinarian visits. The monitoring system comes with a monthly fee.

Heaven's security forces that have played and are playing a role in securing the salvation plan are: God our Father, Jesus His Son, the Holy Spirit, and angels. This level of security measures indicates the real value of that which is being protected. This expresses God's extreme love for us. WOW! In Matthew 18:10, the Bible suggests that our guardian angel reports to Father God of the interpositions made on behalf of His assigned human child of God. I thank God for the unknown number of interpositions and nullification of dangers, seen and unseen.

What noteworthy protection God gives to His believing ones through the divine angels. Listen to the Holy Scriptures regarding the often-unseen guard against the ones who want to do us harm. *"The angel of the LORD encamps around those who fear him, and delivers them" (Psalm 34:7 ESV). "For He will give His angels charge concerning you, to guard you in all your ways" (Psalm 91:11 NASB).*

Reflections

Reflections of your past year, do they haunt you or hug you? Do they harass you or help you? This year manifested itself pregnant with opportunity and great potential. What did you do with your pregnancy? Did you bring it to term and birth it? Did you abort your dream by fear, procrastination, negative self-talk or did you allow negative folks talk you into having an abortion? Were you able to see any personal growth this year? Did your growth appear in a professional manner? Did you see growth in your spiritual life or has your life remained stuck in the same old mud as the previous year?

We all have come up short on reaching our goals, checking off things from our bucket list, and advancing our relationship with God and others. We, perhaps, feel badly. Maybe our lack of progress holds us emotionally hostage to the degree that we look like the "walking depression." We need not stay in this condition. There is hope! The apostle Paul encourages us in this way. *"This one thing I do, forgetting those things which are behind, and reaching forth unto those things which are before, I press toward the mark for the prize of the high calling of God in Christ Jesus"* (Philippians 3:13-14). In other words, we can move forward to new heights and experiences in the coming days accompanied by the power of the Holy Spirit.

As a new season approaches a new page will turn, and a fresh screen will appear. A new or refreshed dream waits to be written. A re-energized you is poised to emerge. So, go ahead and birth that dream, build that business. Employ your talents, skills and abilities in this new season in preparation for an eternity with God. As one Christian communicator challenges, "Educate your mind to love the Bible, to love praising His name, to love the hour of meditation," and talk with God in prayer. As you go forward into this new day with wonderful spiritual aspirations, remember that God wants you to be of earthly good also. As you reflect upon the blessings God bestowed on you, it will motivate you to share the new things that God is doing in you.

I look forward to meeting the new you the next time we meet!

Promises From God

God's promises are true, trustworthy and reliable. We can depend upon the word of God. His promises never fail. His promise to be with us can be seen in the beauty of the sunrise and the clamor of the sunset. Nature's majestic mountains and flowing streams are particular examples of how God blesses our eyes with the splendid scenes of serenity and peace.

Solomon echoes the reliability of God to keep His promises although humans often fail at keeping covenant with God. Solomon, after dedicating the magnificently royal temple in honor of the name of the LORD God of Israel, said this to the people gathered, *"Blessed be the Lord, that hath given rest unto his people Israel, according to all that he promised: there hath not failed one word of all his good promise, which he promised by the hand of Moses his servant"* (1 Kings 8:56).

Not one word of the promises of our God has failed nor can it fail. His very name, *"Immanuel, God with us,"* (Matthew 1:21) has been God's design and desire since Creation. By one man, Adam, sin and separation from God came upon human beings. Yet, Jesus, the Son of the living God, came to redeem the separatist movement and restore the original relationship between divinity and humanity. The word was made flesh and dwelt among us, (and we beheld His glory, the glory as of the only begotten of the Father) full of grace and truth *(John 1:14)*. This God has promised to never leave nor forsake us. Believe it and be blessed even during difficult days! God as well as His promises are reliable, true and trustworthy. Just look around and you will see.

The Merriam-Webster Dictionary defines promise as: "a declaration that one will do or refrain from doing something specified." Michelle Gielan writes that "when we don't keep a promise to someone, it communicates to that person that we don't value him or her. We have chosen to put something else ahead of our commitment. Even when we break small promises, others learn that they cannot count on us." Promises when kept, are the bridges of trust which are essential in a good relationship.

How important are the promises of God to the Christian believer? Hear the Word of the Lord: *"Fear thou not; for I am with thee: be not dismayed; for I am thy God: I will strengthen thee; yea, I will help thee; yea, I will uphold thee with the right hand of my righteousness" (Isaiah 41:10).* *"The LORD shall fight for you, and ye shall hold your peace" (Exodus 14:14).*

God's promises are like water in dry places; oasis in the desert; favorite dessert after a good meal; multicolored flowers decorating a well-worn pathway; high fives and hugs when your day is not the best. One writer declared that "to blot the promises of God from the Word would be like blotting the sun from the sky."

The Long Way Home

He wanted to get home fast. So, he decided to take a shortcut through private property that was clearly marked. The owner had recently purchased two guard dogs to ward off intruders and potential thieves. Heart pumping at a high rate, the little boy scaled the fence and started across the property. Out of nowhere he saw two Rottweilers charging him. Scared! Frightened! He turned to run back to the fence. As he jumped on the fence one of the dogs grabbed his pants leg and tore a gaping hole in his pants. In his frantic state he cut his hand and scratched his knees trying to escape. The short-cut ended up being the longest walk home.

When we make decisions that are totally contrary to the light streaming from the Word of God, it takes longer to recover and reach our destination. The trip took 5 hours and 20 minutes according to Google maps. We were making good time. A friend who had traveled the same route only days before advised us about construction delays. Another friend told us to download the Waze app which provides alternative routes to avoid traffic delays. The app rerouted my wife and I. But we decided to disobey the wisdom of the Waze app, since traffic seemed to be flowing and we didn't want to travel on a two-lane road. The result of our decision delayed our arrival by almost one whole hour.

Decisions may take only a moment to make. The result of the moment of passion, desire or lack of wisdom can make for a long recovery, a longer way home. Life in general, and the Christian life in particular, are fraught with decisions that can lead to safety or danger. The constant credit card and over extending delays postpones financial stability.

The app gives you the choice of choosing the fastest route. The Word of God gives us instruction, information and inspiration to guide us from our house to God's house. As we cooperate with this illumination we will arrive home in the allotted time that the Divine App has sent. *"Thy word is a lamp unto my feet and a light unto my path" (Psalm 119:105).*

Light Living

Since 1986 Tom Bodett's famous line "We'll leave the light on for you" raised Motel 6 in the eye of the traveler. Leaving the light on is a down home indication to guests of your open invitation.

It is of necessity for us to have the light of Heaven's truth to guide our every move. Left to ourselves we bump into things. We will stub our toes in the harrowing darkness of sin. Like driving a car at night, we need to have headlights on to see. A car without its lights on at night is dangerous for that driver and others especially on a dark country road. The scriptures speak to this idea. *"O send out thy light and thy truth: let them lead me; let them bring me unto thy holy hill, and to thy tabernacles" (Psalm 43:3).*

As you travel the dark and dangerous roads of this world, whether you live in the city or the countryside, turn on the light, on high beam if necessary. The light will help you to avoid obstacles in the way, react to sudden moving objects that come out of nowhere. Keep the lights on in order to make it home safely. It was a deep dark night. The clouds covered the moon. The long day of toil and travel drained mother, the driver of the car. Us kids, tired from fighting and arguing and playing sat half asleep in the car. Mother's voice woke us up as we got closer to Grandmamma and Granddaddy's house. That hill blinded our view. Just as we rounded the curve down to the right we saw it. Granddaddy had left the porch light on for us. Remember Jesus is the light that will guide us to His house - His tabernacle - where the redeemed are home at last.

By the way, while we are traversing this pilgrim land, Jesus said that He would leave the light on for us at the Cross, in His church and in the tabernacle of Heaven. This illuminating radiance will never go out because Jesus is the light and the tabernacle all at the same time. *"And I heard a great voice out of heaven saying, Behold, the tabernacle of God is with men, and he will dwell with them, and they shall be his people, and God himself shall be with them, and be their God" (Revelation 21:3).*

New York City is deemed the city that never sleeps. People are afoot at all times throughout the day and night. Yet, there are some who cannot afford a house or apartment. They would accept a single room. The Bible speaks of Jesus dawning His building expertise as He is preparing a place for all who believe in His great salvation *(John 14:1-3).*

"And the city had no need of the sun, neither of the moon, to shine in it: for the glory of God did lighten it, and the Lamb is the light thereof" (Revelation 21:23).

Oh, how I long to dwell in the everlasting light. How about you?

Political Calculus

Is it political calculation, or standing for what's right when government officials insist that a candidate "step aside" and remove himself from the race? Is it simply a public relations strategy or is it doing the right thing when an institution of higher learning suspends three athletes for shoplifting? What constitutes doing the right thing in a day when the moral machinations of our world are offline and stand in need of recalibration?

What does it cost to stand up and speak up for the right side of history? Because the immoral, unethical and sinful nature of humanity pulls so strongly opposing the moral, ethical and righteous force in the world, we tend to give in too easily to our nature. It's as if we are satisfied with taking the path of water - the path of least resistance. Yet, Christian living is a constant struggle between right and wrong. One writer said that it "requires moral courage to do God's work" and not flinch. It is when we choose to place our will on the side of God that we can do the right thing even if we have to stand alone.

My grandfather would describe the manifestation of this type of courage as "Every tub standing on its own bottom." Deciding to do the right thing when the crowd and the masses are skirting, spending and bending the truth takes men, women, boys and girls of moral strength. Solomon writes, *"When the storm has swept by, the wicked are gone, but the righteous stand firm forever" (Proverbs 10:25 NIV).*

When faced with a tough decision remember you are not alone. The Lord is with you as He was with Moses, Daniel, John the Baptist and other historical figures who stood up for God. They took a stand for the right while staring into the face of wrong. Rosa Parks, by taking a seat on that segregated bus in Montgomery, AL in 1951, stood up for the right in the angry face of a dangerous wrong. While others exercise their rights to protest wrong on the football field, in legislative halls, Christians must find the courage to stand up for the right "though the heavens fall."

If you are thinking about quitting, don't. If you are considering giving up, don't. The world needs your tub, young person, stand up against gun violence and for school safety. You can't give up now, my seasoned citizen. The world needs your tub to stand in solidarity with the younger tubs to hold and guide their hands in the new fights against injustice. Therefore, my beloved brethren, be steadfast, unmovable, always abounding in the work of the Lord, forasmuch as ye know that your labor is not in vain in the Lord *(1 Corinthians 15:58).*

Parades

Soon crowds will line the streets of many cities, large and small for their annual 4th of July, Thanksgiving and Christmas Day parades. Marching bands fill the air with the sound of festive music. Cheerleaders from the local high schools compete for attention. Cars and homemade floats covered with artistic renderings from 4H to professional groups follow the path beaten by drum majors, candy throwing clowns and hand shaking politicians. What a fun filled day! Parades are like family photographs when everyone pulls away from life for a brief breath and a smile.

Life in this world is not a parade. This world is a battlefield upon which the great controversy between good and evil is taking place. We must choose which side we will fight on. We must choose which parade we will be in and which drum major we will emulate. Dr. Martin Luther King, Jr. in a sermon entitled, The Drum Major Instinct, called for us to understand the right purpose of being out front. His final analysis was, leaders ought to be servants. His desire to serve can be notarized by the words of this song, "If I can help somebody as I pass along. If I can cheer somebody with a word or song. If I can show somebody he's traveling wrong, then my living will not be in vain. If I can do my duty as a Christian ought. If I can bring salvation to a world once wrought. If I can spread the message as the master taught, then my living will not be in vain."

A choice for good is a choice motivated by the goodness of Jesus. A choice for bad is motivated by negative drum major impulse. Neutrality, is by default, a choice for the evil side.

Success in this warfare is found in siding with Christ and His Spirit. When we choose Jesus, the Holy Spirit comes on the inside of us to work in us the good will of Christ Jesus *(Philippians 2:13)*. With Christ living on the inside we are more than conquerors over lying, backbiting, stealing, sexting. *"Christ in you is the hope of glory" (Colossians 1:27)*.

Soon the golden streets of heaven will be lined with Holy Angels waving signs of welcome to Paradise. Wonderful and exhilarating music fills the heavens as the Redeemed from the earth are home at last. The lame will start running and leaping and praising God. The blind see bright yellows and all shades of beautiful blue without the aid of the super expensive technology of the electronic glasses. The tongue of the deaf and dumb are loosed so they can sing and shout the victory.

Suddenly we all stand at parade rest. The Captain of the Lord of Hosts rises above the sea of saints. What wonder! What majesty, splendor and illuminating glory! We all fall on our knees and worship Him. With raised hands scarred by nails Jesus declares in a loving yet royal tone, "Well done, good and faithful servants. Enter into the joy of your Lord". We stand and shout, "Glory! Hallelujah to our God!" Instead of candy, Jesus hands out crowns of life! *(Revelation 2:10)*

Principles of Fun

We may debate the rightness or wrongness of musical genres, movie content, whether Christians should be involved in the political process - vote or hold an office.

Some folks frown upon all amusements even the innocent laughter of a child. Still others live, eat and breathe for the intoxicant called pleasure. How can we know what's appropriate or not? Are there any guiding principles for us to take in? Here are a few principles that you may find helpful. The following six criteria for appropriate amusement and recreational pleasures adapted from E. G. White's religious reading entitled *My Life Today*:

1. Not pleasure-inducing only
   Will pleasure-seeking be the only participatory benefit?
2. Not mind-squandering
   Will this amusement be dissipating to my mind?
3. Not soul-debasing
   Will the amusement or recreation be demeaning, corrupting to my character?
4. Doesn't leave a bad after-taste
   Will it leave a bad taste in my mouth/heart after the thrill is gone?
5. Not self-respect destroying
   Will it destroy self-respect and my influence on others?

6. Jesus-friendly
   Is it Jesus-friendly? Can I invite Jesus to tag along with me?

The Scriptures employ us to be principled thinkers on the subject of recreation and amusement. Therefore, by the power of the indwelling Christ, let's enjoy life as God gives it to us. Christ has already lived the perfect principled life for us. It is ours by faith. Faith and fun aren't necessarily dichotomous.

"Finally, brethren, whatsoever things are true, whatsoever things are honest, whatsoever things are just, whatsoever things are pure, whatsoever things are lovely, whatsoever things are of good report; if there be any virtue, and if there be any praise, think on these things" (Philippians 4:8).

Make It Count

Accountability is a tough word in our society. Accountability is a strange word for many people. Some get away with not being accountable to the regulations and rules of engagement. When a presidential candidate mocks an individual with a disability and does not apologize, accountability is wanting. When we don't take offense to ridiculous societal behavior, true accountability is lacking.

So, accountability or the lack thereof can be viewed from an individual and corporate platform. The student, not his parent or friend, is responsible for doing the work assigned by the teacher or professor. Playing point guard on a basketball team carries a particular amount of accountability. An assembly line worker needs to do a good job because the down line workers rely on it.

Each person is responsible and accountable to God for the unique work that has been divinely assigned. You, sir, you, ma'am, are wired by the creative genius of Our God to discover, develop and deploy your gifts and giftedness into the world. Withholding because of fear, and insecurity is not a valid excuse for robbing the community, the church and God. The Lord God entrusted you with gifts and talents, therefore, use them for humanitarian uplift and for His glory.

Corporate repentance is sometimes in order when the agency, organization or church has mistreated, maligned and molested their mission, message and the many. In manufacturing the company issues a "recall" admitting their transgressions. Daniel, the Old Testament prophet, offers a clear statement of a corporate repentance in prayer to Jehovah by saying, *"we have sinned" (Daniel 9:15)* even though he had not personally participated.

Maybe it's time for us to repent individually and corporately. Are there areas in your life that you need to say to God, "I'm sorry?" Is it time for your denomination, diocese, general assembly or local congregation to repent of any member malfeasance, mission malfunction or miscommunication of the message of Christ?

It is time for Christians to embrace the fact that we have fallen way short, in our own strength, in representing the character of God in the world. If we believe these things to be so, I employ you to recall the Savior's disposition to us and desire for us:

"The Lord is not slack concerning his promise, as some men count slackness; but is longsuffering to us-ward, not willing that any should perish, but that all should come to repentance" (2 Peter 3:9 KJV).

Which One?

Which is worth more, a handbag made by hand or a purse produced by MK? Which is more valuable, a political sermon or a pastoral speech? Which is more captivating, an episode of *The Haves and the Have Nots* or understanding the great controversy between Christ and Satan? Which would you rather have, ten golden eggs or the goose that lays golden eggs?

Making choices without full knowledge or gaining more facts about the item or situation is not wise. My Granddaddy taught us to value money in a crude game. On our visits he would sometimes give us as my father used to say, "a piece of money." The lesson game went like this. He would hold two coins in his hand and ask us to choose which one we wanted. Without telling us the value of the coins we had to choose between the "little nickel" – the real nickel – and the "big nickel" – the quarter. As kids we quickly picked the quarter because it was bigger. He then told us the value of our choice and we were happy. Then one day he had more money for us. We had to choose between the "shiny penny" – the dime – or the "little nickel." Again, as kids we picked the "little nickel" because it was bigger. Then Granddaddy had to tell us the value of our choices. I am thankful to have learned that bigger does not always mean greater in value.

Through his object lesson many a wise man talked about learning the value of a thing. People talk about a lot of things. Living in this world it's impossible not to have a dialogue about the budget, the car repairs, the high price of food and gas, religion and health insurance. Sports is another topic which dominates the airwaves in the barber shop. Yet, there are topics of weightier value and substance. Myles Munroe observed that conversation is polarized by one's status in life. He said, "Poor people talk about money all the time, rich people talk about things. Wealthy people, they talk about ideas."

One of my favorite authors offers other topics worthy and valuable enough for conversation when people gather together. Such topics will bring animation and invigoration to the downward, depressing debate about the state of our World. Ellen White encourages that we talk about, "The love of Jesus, the salvation offered to fallen man through His infinite love, holiness of heart, the precious, saving truth for these last days, the grace of Jesus Christ."

The hymnologist wrote, "Let's talk about Jesus, the King of kings is He. The Lord of lords supreme, through all eternity. The great I AM, the Way, the Truth, the Life, the Door. Let's talk about Jesus more and more."

"Let your conversation be always full of grace, seasoned with salt, so that you may know how to answer everyone" (Colossians 4:6).

Which one is worth more of your talk, the "big nickel" or the Cross? You decide.

"The Youth"

"Oh, the youth, the youth," is the cry of anger, frustration and exasperation. Juvenile courts and detention centers in many metropolitan areas of the USA are crowded. Why are we being forced to face this mounting problem along with other related concerns? Once upon a time he wore a diaper and dawned the biggest smile. Things were going great. Now he is facing a judge and a system that doesn't remember the diaper or the boy who once looked at the future with hope. Now, all they see is an "at-risk" youth, a troublemaker, and a potential number for the correctional system that disproportionately incarcerates men of color which comprise 56% of the prison population as cited by the National Association for the Advancement of Colored People.

Confused by his own developing brain, he doesn't always make the best emotional, rational decisions. Many of which are made because of the underlying need to be accepted by peers. So, the alluring pull of the wrong, the evil, in this world grabs at our growing, independence seeking youth. The once happy kid is now angry at his or her parents, perplexed at friends who don't seem to understand and is undeniably mad at the Institutions, including the church, that let him or her become a statistic rather than be seen as a person.

David Kinnaman of the Barna Research Group observes that the youth ages 15 to 29 are leaving or have already left the church for the following six reasons:

- Isolationistic nature of the church is problematic.

- Shallowness or lack of relevancy is their view of the church's God.
- Anti-science is how the youth see the posture of the church.
- Sex and the church's policy of just say no is not enough.
- Exclusivity of the church against the pluralism of their friends is challenging.
- Doubters of the church's doctrinal positions are not welcomed.

How shall we deal with this dilemma? Do we drift into our separate corners and never more to meet again? Kinnaman suggests that we discard the "passing the baton" picture and find ways to blend the old with the young for a more comprehensive ministry. My Granddaddy would agree with Kinnaman. I recall him saying that the "old folks and the young bucks gotta' work together."

What would happen if "many" simple smiles, kind words and love shown to our at-risk youth who walk our streets, wake up in our homes and worship in our sanctuaries? What would happen if we opened our hearts, homes and houses of worship as places of positive promise? To those over 40, what if we cried not out of frustration and angst but out of love and concern "Oh, our youth, our youth?"

Peter agreed with the prophet Joel regarding the blending of youthful energy and mature wisdom. *"And it shall come to pass in the last days, saith God, I will pour out of my Spirit upon all flesh: and your sons and your daughters shall prophesy, and your young men shall see visions, and your old men shall dream dreams: And on my servants and on my handmaidens I will pour out in those days of my Spirit; and they shall prophesy" (Acts 2:17).*

Gold Rules

What gold rules your home? Is it the Golden Rule or is it the rule of gold?

If it's the Rule of Gold then your house may look like this:

- Work - in early; out late
- Things - valued more than people
- Little or no time for others

"For the love of money is a root of all sorts of evil, and some by longing for it have wandered away from the faith and pierced themselves with many griefs" (1 Timothy 6:10 NASB).

If your house values The Golden Rule then it may look, sound and feel like this:

- Neat, clean, smiles...
- Please, thank you...
- Hugs, kisses, kindness...

"Do to others whatever you would like them to do to you. This is the essence of all that is taught in the law and the prophets" (Matthew 7:12 NLT).

Relationship with Jesus in a house where gold rules looks like this:

"The whole transaction of religious conversion has been made mechanical and spiritless...Christ may be 'received' without creating any special love for Him in the soul of the receiver. The man is 'saved' but he is not hungry and thirsty after God," says the 20th century Christian scholar, A. W. Tozer.

We don't want to be gold diggers, in it for the transactional blessings, and benefits. We must know that we are loved first by an awesome God and that this Deity wants to bless us – load us up with daily benefits *(Psalm 68:19)*. God with tremendous grace gives us the breath to breathe, eyes to see, food to eat. To such we should learn to pray like the matured believers such as my Granddaddy whose prayers often included thanksgiving for "a reasonable portion of health and strength." Receive him today and he will add all these things and more unto you. Allured and drawn by Heaven's great, mighty and awesome love we respond to God and others from the positional understanding of love. Our actions and behaviors to others will be for their good because we value them, not their things or what we can get out of them. We value others because God created them in His image.

"The life of a church cannot be sustained by hard work, right living and doctrinal correctness. The life of the church, the life of a Christian, lies in our love for Christ which reflects His great love for us," says Colin Smith. What an awesome perspective. God is always looking out for us. God will even impregnate your trouble with an unreasonable portion of faith and hope *(Jeremiah 29:11)*.

The Gospel thinks of others before self.

He Hit Me First

Growing up in the "neighborhood" Mama's advice was, "don't start any fights, but if they hit you first, hit back." You probably received the same cautionary instructions. These instructions of self-defense helped one survive. However, a few years ago there was an escalation in thuggish, cowardice and horrifying sucker punching. Many filmed these horrendous attacks of the so called "knockout" games then placed them on YouTube and other social media platforms for thousands, yeah millions to see. In 2015 an eighteen-year-old in the Paterson, New Jersey area, walks up to a much older gentleman at the street corner and gains his attention. Looks in the camera and says something. He laughs then sucker punches this older man who is later hospitalized for several days.

Surviving in the spiritual "hood," causes one to fight a different kind of fight. This battle calls for offensive and defensive strategies. A helpful defensive strategy is in the utilization of prayer and Bible reading to sharpen the mind and guard the heart. Recall Paul's outstanding pastoral counsel to the church at Philippi, *"Do not be anxious about anything, but in everything by prayer and supplication with thanksgiving let your requests be made known to God. And the peace of God, which surpasses all understanding, will guard your hearts and your minds in Christ Jesus"* (Philippians 4:6-7).

Walking in the streets of this world one must be visually and mentally alert at all times. Satan, the captain of the evil hosts, likes to sucker punch people by pushing "people from one extreme to the other." Life's going well and seemingly out of nowhere comes an illness, joblessness, divorce or even death. It's here that we raise our offensive weapons and hit back. The weapons are the same as the defensive ones, yet we deploy them in a more aggressive and tactical manner. Directed prayers become as guided missiles. Believers in faith hurl Bible verses at their perplexities and trials confident that victory will come. Standing on the promises of God's holy word, they develop a "cultivated, cheerful, happy spirit" that trusts in the Captain of the Heavenly Hosts.

The New Jersey sucker puncher confessed to the crime before a judge and received punishment. The courts won and justice prevailed. In the final showdown between good and evil, Satan will be brought low and "at the name of Jesus every knee should bow of things in heaven and things in the earth and things under the earth and every tongue should confess that Jesus Christ is Lord" (Philippians 2:10-11). No sucker punches needed.

In Christ and with Christ we are *"MORE THAN CONQUERORS" (Romans 8:34)*.

Look! Did You See That?

Yesteryear was the time of colorful arrangement of black and white. Church folks wore these colors with pride and honor. In 20th century America, clergy dressed in a crisp black suit and tie accented with a sharply pressed white shirt and shiny black shoes. Ushers adorned themselves with the unchangeable contrast - black skirt and white blouse. Early 19th century American theatre popularized the minstrel where white actors covered their faces black and lampooned the plight of blacks through buffoonery. The days of such stark contrast are gone, yet their residue in many respects remains.

Today, color contrast is more dynamic. It evolved into an accepted cacophony of loud and soft colors, prints and patterns. It is into this ever-changing environment that the Christ-centered Christian walks with a steady stream of truth and love. Like Jesus we are bold, but not brash, concerning the truth. The apostle Paul was firm on principles of truth, but ever thoughtful and courteous in the communication thereof.

Our world seems to be overrun with dark images of violence, abuse and hatred. These pictures of sin cascade the news reports on a daily, hourly basis. Peter whose life was drastically changed by the love of Jesus desired to see this video, *"Finally, be ye all of one mind, having compassion one of another, love as brethren, be pitiful, be courteous"* (1 Peter 3:8).

Fellow Christians, our call is to be a pleasant and powerful blend of truth and love, bold and beautiful, conviction and courtesy, holy and happy. Such a life comes only by beholding the Christ and lifting Him up before the world by the Spirit's power. What does that look like?

Look! Do you see that Christian mixing and matching while standing firm for and with Jesus? I see millennial and seasoned saints serving disaster affected communities. I see their lives being changed by gospel truth as it is in Jesus. They are, as one man prayed, "being saved by the same gospel they take to others." What a special blend of youth and years! Do you see it too? Is it just my imagination, running away with me?

Right now, we see this prescriptive organization only with low visibility. However, the prophetic descriptive will allow the highly visible people of God to do ministry on a much higher plane than ever seen before. This Church coalescing around the Cross is the breath of fresh air that the world needs to see. Arise and shine for your light has come. The day will soon come and the prophetic vision of Joel, young and old collaborating for the glory of God, will be a wonderful reality.

Minstrels light up the stage with a song and a dance. Messengers light up the world with a message. Jesus said of His Church, *"You are the light of the world. A city set on a hill cannot be hidden" (Matthew 5:14 ESV)*.

The Elegance of a Christian; Courtesy Counts

Courtesy is something of a lost art in our day. One would be hard pressed to find politeness of manners and civility consistently practiced in our daily culture. Political analysts and candidates often behave in ways that are less than polite. Athletes often engage in trash talking which makes for great drama but distracts from good sportsmanship. Life's most precious and memorable moments are lost and squandered because someone failed to be courteous.

Religions of varying stripes have taught for centuries the notion that expectation of reciprocity starts with how you treat others. Doing to others what you would have them do to you is The Golden Rule. The Bible teaches us to look out for and lavish love upon one another (John 13:34). Chick-fil-A restauranteur, Dan Cathy, believes that customer courtesy is born on the backs of "humility, passion for service, compassion, and genuineness." The expectation of all employees at Mr. Cathy's fast food restaurants is to make extraordinary customer courtesy while serving up good food at the same time.

Abraham was a courtesy believer and worshipper of Jehovah God. In a dispute over grazing land for his flock, he chose the more barren and challenging land and gave Lot the best. Abraham practiced courtesy among his family. Abraham's house became "the little hotel on the side of the road" where weary travelers got food and rest. By opening his home to travelers, he expressed and released the kindness of his heart.

Abraham showed courtesy and amazing honesty in business. He insisted on talking with the appropriate owner of the real estate and negotiated to pay full price for buying a burial spot for Sarah even though he could have drove a hard bargain. Abraham, while not perfect, is a good example of one who practiced courtesy in the affairs of day to day life. Can you name areas in your life where the elegance of courtesy needs more practice? It would be something as simple as saying please, thank you, excuse me or opening the door for the person in front of you. What if the older taught the younger the how and the why of practicing politeness and good manners?

Remember what the Word of God says, *"But love your enemies, and do good, and lend, expecting nothing in return; and your reward will be great, and you will be sons of the Most High; for He Himself is kind to ungrateful and evil men" (Luke 6:35).*

"Do what the Good Book says" are the echoing words from my sage and granddad. The Good Book, the Bible, says in the Contemporary English Translation *"Treat others as you want them to treat you" (Matthew 7:12).*

Social to Save

Jesus did not stand aloof and detached from the people. He socialized with them, even if they differed in some theological point. Christ exercised consistent kindness and honest truth telling at the same time. Jesus always couched His truth telling and caring deeds in love. This approach allowed Jesus to speak into, to uplift and impact the lives of many.

What is your approach in dealing with people who philosophically, ideologically, theologically disagree with your assessment of the matter in question? What do you do when your spouse's views are a bit more liberal than yours? How do you respond when your co-worker determines that your understanding of the Bible or religion is suspect or wrong?

Regarding *Homo sapiens*, my wise old granddaddy gave me this piece of advice as I prepared for ministry. He said, "Wherever you go just remember that people will always be people. You gotta learn how to deal with them." Here's what I know and offer for your consideration.

1. Don't argue (fight) or debate the Bible with people. Learn to listen and share your thoughts and allow the Holy Spirit to convince, convict and convert.

2. Don't demonize those who disagree with you. Your understanding of truth and life while good can always be better. Remember what the

seasoned saints used to say, "You can catch more flies with honey than with vinegar."

3. Don't be a politician who spouts rash rhetoric against the opponent for public display in order to score points with the base. Remember: *A gentle answer turns away wrath, but a harsh word stirs up anger (Proverbs 15:1).*

4. Stand for something not just against something. One of my ministerial mentors told me, "It's better to have folks respect you than to have them like you."

Jesus is our example in all things. Let's seek to be like Jesus. He went about doing good. The Gospel is to be given in "word and deed." Look at how the apostle John admonishes us to display the dual action of the Gospel; *"Dear children, let's not merely say that we love each other; let us show the truth by our actions" (1 John 3:18).*

A difference in doctrine and faith doesn't mean they are the "devil." But what we think, say and do to them will identify if we are of the devil or of Christ.

"This is my commandment, That ye love one another, as I have loved you" (John 15:12). This is the word of the Lord Jesus.

Little Foxes

I remember. It was in my seventh-grade science class that we looked through the microscope and saw the awesome, intricate and exquisite details of a flower's petal. I was intrigued and amazed at that which was hidden from the naked eye - wow. However, the amazement diminished when the teacher said that what we examined under the microscope would be on the next test.

Small things matter in life. "Cleanup after yourself", was a phrase that my mother often repeated. Why, because small things matter. "The basic fundamental things win basketball games. Defense - stay between your man and the basket, slide your feet and rebound the basketball. Offense - dribble, pass (look for the open man), follow through on your shot and rebound." These were the words of my high school basketball coach.

A kind word, a response tempered by grace, a helping hand, on-time payments, following through on your commitments matters. Little things done in the right spirit can magnify or minimize a marriage. Husbands take note that while she remembers that big gift she appreciates the small things more. Women take note as well that your husband responds better when you stroke his ego in small consistent doses. *"A gentle answer turns away wrath, but a harsh word stirs up anger,"* is the wisdom Solomon shares (Proverbs 15:1).

The legendary UCLA basketball coach, John Wooden observed, "It's the little details that are vital. Little things make big things happen." If folks who profess to be

Christians would consistently read a little of the Bible, pray simple but meaningful prayers and serve humanity a little more without any strings attached, the world would be a little better place. *"Do not forget to do good and to share with others, for with such sacrifices God is pleased" (Hebrews 13:16 NIV).*

Lest we forget this impactful remark, "It is the little things of life that develop the spirit in men and women and determine the character." Take us the foxes, the little foxes, that spoil the vines *(Song of Solomon 2:15).*

Remember, it is the little things in life that matter. Others, long after you have forgotten, will remember the kind words, the thoughtful gestures. Thanks for reading.

Love: Protects and Promotes

Someone said, "Blood is thicker than water." The conventional meaning of this colloquial proverb has to do with family relationships being closer than friendship bonds. This is a true statement and we ought to behave in that way. Blood has viscosity, thickness. The viscosity of the blood helps in clotting which prevents hemorrhaging.

Trouble attacked the Republicans congressional baseball team. It was on June 14, 2017, at Eugene Simpson Stadium Park in Alexandria, Virginia when an angry man opened gunfire on the unsuspecting players on the practice field. Congressman Steve Scalise from Louisiana was seriously injured but has since recovered. The Speaker of the House, Paul Ryan of Wisconsin said, "An attack on one is an attack on all." This ought to be the sentiment of all families and the members thereof.

Trouble, like an approaching rain, was brewing in the wind. Some boy inappropriately put his hands on our youngest sister. Two older brothers and I ran to the scene of the crime. It was there that street justice prevailed in the 'hood'. Let's say that the principle of nonviolence purported by Dr. Martin Luther King, Jr. took a beating that day. The high blood pressure of disrespect won. Our reaction to regain respect failed to consider that "Hate cannot drive out hate, only love can do that."

Love simply displayed in the family circle will serve as a protective force-field and perimeter against attackers. More importantly, family love, godly love, nurtures and builds character. Love adds value and values others. Real love fosters a nurturing disposition for those in the house and outside of the house. The apostle Paul writing to the church in Corinth declares that love *"always protects, always trusts, always hopes, always perseveres" (1 Corinthians 13:7 NIV)*.

"Dear friends, let us love one another, for love comes from God. Everyone who loves has been born of God and knows God" (1 John 4:7 NIV).

Let this be our goal. Like "blood" let's coalesce, come close and connect. How we love and who we love today, will matter tomorrow.

Secret to Happiness

Every person, individual, man woman or child seeks, desires and craves happiness. Yet, we humans often try to earn or buy while our hearts and emotional tanks remain below the warning line. The last place you looked was unsuccessful. Now, your tank registers empty and you are running off fumes from last week's fill up. Finding happiness seems to be elusive and slippery at best.

One solution is work. While researchers believe work – meaningful work is a part of the happiness formula, working harder and remaining in poverty does not bring happiness with it. Moreover, making more money to move one out of poverty does move the happiness meter, according to Arthur C. Brooks of the New York Times.

Solution number two is to work more efficient. I like Star Trek and the subsequent shows which followed such as Star Trek Voyager. In this series the character 7 of 9, a former Borg drone who is transitioning into becoming human again, operates with machine-like precision. 7 of 9 often rags on the shortcomings of her human colleagues of Star Fleet by stating their failed attempts as, "Inefficient." Today we try to capture happiness by assimilating more technology and automation. We seek to be more efficient and productive so that we can buy better things and be proud of ourselves. This doesn't seem to work. We end up empty and exhausted.

A third solution is to invite Jesus into your life as an honored and abiding guest. Guests tend to have an energizing effect on us. We clean more. We cook more. We do more when we know that guests are coming. Our conversation is different when guests are abiding in the house. Just imagine what could happen, what would happen if Jesus Christ was invited in as a permanent abiding resident into our lives. We would treat others right. We would live to please our live-in Guest. Finally, God would be pleased to invite us to reside and abide with Him for eternity.

The secret to finding happiness is as singer Larnelle Harris suggests, "it's not in trying but in trusting" and "not in running but in resting" in the comforting company of the Lord. Ellen White remarks, "That heart is the happiest that has Christ as an abiding guest."

Glory ye in his holy name: let the heart of them rejoice that seek the Lord (1 Chronicles 16:10).

Never Say Goodbye

Good bye, see you later, later dude, holly atcha, are terms of temporary disconnection between persons. This disconnect is with the hope of again seeing others face to face, talking on the phone or video transmission via an available technological platform such as FaceTime. The closer the relationship often determines how soon the desire for reconnection. Separation anxiety increases based on the mutual fondness.

Teenagers who believe that they are in love can hardly stand to be apart. Their separation anxiety was greater a few years ago when teenage love had to wait until after class to walk down the hall to see each other or wait until mother was off the house telephone to call. Today, they each have a cell phone and they can connect with a text message, a tweet on Twitter or video messages on Snap chat or Facebook any time of the day.

Our visit came to an end. We all made our way to the front door ready to walk across the wooden porch down those steps and toward the car. In doing this I remember my grandfather's goodbye would go like this, *"Ya'll come back and see me. Ya hear."* At first, I only thought this was just his way of saying goodbye or see you later. Now that he's separated from us and asleep in death awaiting the resurrection, I find myself visiting him from time to time and with vivid memories of him donning his creased overalls, light blue shirt, black shoes and hat. I can hear his voice speaking words of wisdom from a past age to a generation that can benefit from an ear to hear. Titus hears a similar mentoring voice of the apostle when Paul instructs the younger pastor in how to lead his congregation and close the generation gaps. Here is a sample of Paul's counsel regarding men to boys mentoring; *"Similarly, encourage the young men to be self-controlled. In everything set them an example by doing what is good. In your teaching show integrity, seriousness and soundness of speech that cannot be condemned, so that those who oppose you may be ashamed because they have nothing bad to say about us" (Titus 2:6-8).*

Jesus told his disciples good bye. I will see you soon. Before dying on the cross as humanity's sin sacrifice Jesus gathered the 11 around him adding, *"Let not your heart be troubled: ye believe in God, believe also in me. In my Father's house are many mansions: if it were not so, I would have told you. I go to prepare a place for you. And if I go and prepare a place for you, I will come again, and receive you unto myself; that where I am, there ye may be also" (John 14:1-3).*

While some may say, "Come back to see me." I think I like the notion of Jesus saying, "I'll be back to get you, soon." While we wait for The Lord Jesus to return let's live with integrity, honesty, temperance and love, so practical, Godly wisdom can travel from Generation to Generation.

ABOUT THE AUTHOR

DR. FRED W. BATTEN, JR. is the Senior Pastor of the Word of Life Seventh-day Adventist Church in Memphis, Tennessee. He holds a Bachelor of Arts Degree in Business Administration from Middle Tennessee State University, Murfreesboro, Tennessee, Master of Theological Studies Degree from Vanderbilt Divinity School, Nashville, Tennessee, Doctor of Ministries Degree (with a concentration in Urban Ministries), from Andrews University, Berrien Springs, Michigan.

As a certified Leadership Coach, Teacher and Speaker with the John Maxwell Team, he helps churches and organizations with leadership essentials. Dr. Batten hosted a radio broadcast for 10 years entitled "FYI - For Your Inspiration". His eighteen years of full-time ministry with the Seventh-day Adventist Church began in the Mississippi Delta, Jackson and Canton Mississippi and presently Memphis Tennessee. He helped to organize the Disaster Response and Long-Term Recovery efforts in Jackson, MS after Hurricane Katrina. Dr. Batten serves on the Spiritual Wellness Council of the Regional One Hospital in Memphis, Tennessee. He has traveled as an international speaker and trainer.

As pastor of the Word of Life Seventh-day Adventist Church in Memphis, the church has continued to enlarge its community presence with homework diner, Volunteer Income Tax Assistance (VITA), community block parties and ministry to the elderly. Dr. Batten enjoys reading on a variety of subjects. He likes to watch Star Trek, old western episodes like Bonanza and Gunsmoke. He also enjoys watching football, playing basketball and tennis. Dr. Batten works to add value, share wisdom and impart the Gospel to all generations. Dr. Batten and his wife, Denise, are the proud parents of two adult daughters. Amber, who graduated from Oakwood University with a Registered Nurse degree, and Brandi who is pursuing a master's degree in Clinical Mental Health Counseling.

One generation shall praise Your works to another.

-Psalm 145:4, NASB

CONNECT WITH AUTHOR

Dr. Fred W. Batten, Jr.

EMAIL: DRFBATTENJR@gmail.com

WEBSITE: www.drfredbatten.com

www.ingramcontent.com/pod-product-compliance
Lightning Source LLC
Chambersburg PA
CBHW052155110526
44591CB00012B/1967